Dedication

This book is dedicated to all of the police administrators, upper command, supervisors, and officers who took risks with implementing and practicing community policing. You often met resistance, were ridiculed, and even forced to leave the department because of your commitment to providing community policing services to those citizens you served.

We salute you!

Community Policing

How to Get Started

Robert Trojanowicz

Director, National Center for Community Policing
Professor, Urban Affairs Programs
Michigan State University

Bonnie Bucqueroux

Associate Director, National Center for Community Policing
Michigan State University

anderson publishing co.
p.o. box 1576
cincinnati, oh 45201-1576
(513) 421-4142

Community Policing: How to Get Started

ISBN: 0-87084-874-7
Library of Congress Catalog Number: 93-79363

 The text of this book is printed on recycled paper.

Kelly Humble *Managing Editor*   Cover photos courtesy of the Lansing (MI) Police Department

Hugo's adage "Stronger than an army is an idea whose time has come" accurately describes the philosophy of community policing in the 1990s. The lack of confidence in America's criminal justice system and the economic dilemma currently facing most American cities has created the need for viable alternatives to "reactive," or traditional, policing. This publication bridges the gap between "new ideas" of community policing and the implementation of new police procedures and practice.

Community policing is an innovative and more powerful way of focusing a police department's energies and talents on the underlying conditions that often give rise to crime and repeated calls for police assistance. With the exception of certain types of "directed patrol," traditional policing employs an incident-driven style—handling each incident as if it had neither a past nor a future related to other neighborhood issues or incidents in the community. By contrast, community policing challenges a department to employ a wider range of tactics and strategies rather than simply rushing to the scene of all reported crimes simply to take a report on a long-gone culprit. Community policing helps police officers and community-based collaborators analyze the reasons that certain incidents arise and helps them devise interventions that will reduce some of the underlying causes. Community policing expands the police officer's "medic bag" significantly by replacing some of the "band-aids" with effective diagnostic, curative, and preventive tools.

While community policing is not a panacea, it promotes mutual trust and cooperation between citizens and police. As the authors state, it helps to empower neighborhoods in danger of being overwhelmed by crime, drugs, and the poisonous mix of apathy, despair and unrest.

There is an air of impoverished drabness, of tired routine, of stagnant monotony in most police functions, but it has been focused in the lack of insight surrounding the causes of crime. The symptoms of the illness afflicting America's police involve conformity and timidity and are expressed by reliance on past practice. However, this is not meant to diminish the day-to-day contributions to public safety that the vast majority of dedicated and hard working police officers make.

Community policing is becoming the operating philosophy in a growing number of police agencies of all sizes throughout the United States and is the productive change that America's communities and neighborhoods need. It is both a philosophy and an organizational strategy that allows the police and community residents to work closely together in new ways to solve the problems of crime, physical and social disorder, and neighborhood decay. The philosophy rests on the belief that citizens in the community deserve input into the police process in exchange for their participation and support. It also rests on the belief that solutions to contemporary community problems demand freeing both citizens and the police to explore creative, new ways to address neighborhood concerns beyond a narrow focus on individual crime incidents.

The authors make a substantial contribution to community policing by developing a hands-on, practical approach to the implementation of the community policing philosophy. By outlining a clear definition of community policing, the authors have laid a foundation that allows the implementation of community policing practices to be developed and easily understood—putting theory into practice.

Robert C. Wadman
Chief of Police
Wilmington Police Department
Wilmington, North Carolina

Community policing is being touted by some as the cure-all for the problems within and without the criminal justice system. However, it is not a panacea. There are many obstacles and challenges to community policing becoming a viable catalyst for changing public policy in the future.

Since its inception in 1983, the National Center for Community Policing at Michigan State University has conducted several training sessions, both on and off campus, and has provided technical assistance to numerous communities. The Center has also continued to conduct research and disseminate information via such mechanisms as the *Footprints* newsletter and the *Community Policing Series*. The Charles Stewart Mott foundation provided funding for many of the activities.

The Center has been contacted more than 8,000 times by people seeking information and assistance. Increasingly, police officers and officials have said that they are either doing community policing or are about to begin participating in it. However, there is some question as to whether some of these efforts reflect the necessary elements of community policing or are merely reactions to a contemporary political thrust for police reform. Is community policing just a contemporary "buzz" word with no long-term commitment?

Because of the different perceptions about community policing and the wide variations in its implementation, staff of the Center and staff of the Behavioral Sciences Unit of the Federal Bureau of Investigation have conducted a nationwide survey of all departments that have at least 100 sworn officers or serve populations of more than 50,000 to determine if they are doing community policing, and if so, according to what definition. The return rate of the 17-page questionnaire has been greater than 80 percent, and the results will be shared in a forthcoming publication. There will also be a follow-up questionnaire to sample jurisdictions smaller than 50,000, which represent the vast majority of cities and towns in the United States.

Regardless of how community policing is implemented, its basic elements must be identified so that the community policing officer will have reference points and procedures for carrying out tasks. This book is not meant to provide an answer to every specific contingency that may occur in every community that is implementing or embarking on the journey to implement community policing. Rather, this is an attempt to provide the reference points and logical steps necessary to make community policing a viable reality. In other words, this publication attempts to provide the "skeleton." The specific actors in the community will need to put the "meat on the bones" so that the approach meets the needs of the particular jurisdiction.

This book has been divided into seven sections, with most followed by questions and answers. These questions and answers are the result of queries to the staff at the Center over the years from hundreds of people interested in community policing. Obviously these are not the only questions that may arise and, likewise, these are not necessarily the only answers. Two examples of commonly asked questions and their "answers" are provided below.

> *At what speed should a police department proceed in order for community policing to be effective?* The department should progress fast enough so that it creates enough tension for change to take place, but not so fast that there is irreparable animosity among the key players. Such animosity could develop between the community policing officer and his or her sergeant, the community policing officer and "regular" motor officers, the department and political leaders, or the department and citizens who are not initially the recipients of the personalized services of community policing. It is like fishing—keeping enough tension on the line to reel in the fish, but not so much tension that the line breaks.

As shown in the above example, an answer may not address the question in absolute terms but may provide a helpful guideline. Other answers may be more definitive:

> *Is permanent assignment of an officer to an area necessary for community policing to be effective?* Permanency (at least 18 months) is necessary so that the officer gets to be known by name, so that trust is established and long-term solutions to problems can take place.

The sections of this book range from the theory and definition of community policing, to the actual duties of the officer, to supervising and evaluating the officer. It is surely not the last word on the subject. Community policing will continue to evolve.

We would like to acknowledge the following people for their assistance with this project: Bruce Benson, Andrew George, Elaine Hoekwaker, Gene Hoekwaker, Tina McLanus, Armilla Simon, Ron Sloan, David Sinclair, Elise Trojanowicz, Susan Trojanowicz, and DeVere Woods.

Contents

Section Two
The Planning Process:
A Community Policing Approach to Change

Section Three
Understanding and Involving the Community

Section Four
Preparing the Department   55

Section Five
What Community Policing Officers Do on the Job   75

Section Six
Supervising and Evaluating Community Policing Officers   97

What is Community Policing?

The Challenge of Defining Community Policing

Community policing has made the transition from being a promising experiment to becoming the wave of the future. Recent research conducted by the National Center for Community Policing in cooperation with the FBI Academy's Behavioral Sciences Unit verified earlier findings that the majority of police departments in major jurisdictions have already adopted some form of community policing reform, or they plan to do so in the near future.

Yet confusion persists concerning precisely what community policing is. What definition are departments using when they claim to be doing community policing?

Is community policing only a philosophy—a new way of thinking? Or must police also change what they do—adopting a new organizational strategy? Is community policing merely a new program, based on stationing community policing officers in beats in high-crime neighborhoods? Or does it require changes in the way that all police personnel, civilian and sworn, interact with and deliver services to the community?

Is community policing just a name for what the best police departments have been doing all along? Is it just another name for problem-solving/problem-oriented policing? How does it differ from other programs, such as crime prevention and police-community relations? Does it turn police officers into social workers?

Community policing's ultimate success or failure rests on reaching a consensus about what the concept of community policing means. If the definition is too vague, then too many programs qualify as already participating in community policing, and it is therefore perceived as requiring no substantive change. And if competing definitions persist, the term is rendered meaningless. It is time to draw clear lines between what community policing is—and what it is not.

This section will define community policing in various ways, to serve different needs. There will be times, such as when a TV reporter thrusts a microphone in front of you and there is no time for detail, that a broad definition serves the purpose. In training sessions or in community meetings, a definition that can both educate and inspire is often needed.

When it comes time to write concrete plans to implement community policing, you will need to grasp the nuances required to explore how and why community policing should be adopted as a city-wide (jurisdiction-wide) strategy with a department-wide commitment.

The Big Six

The Big Six refers to the six groups that must be identified and work together to ensure the success of any community policing efforts.

1. **The Police Department**—including all personnel, from the chief to the line officer, civilian and sworn.

2. **The Community**—including everyone, from formal and informal community leaders such as presidents of civic groups, ministers, and educators; to community organizers and activities; to average citizens on the street.

3. **Elected Civic Officials**—including the mayor, city manager, city council, and any county, state, and federal officials whose support can affect community policing's future.

4. **The Business Community**—including the full range of businesses, from major corporations to the "Mom & Pop" store on the corner.

5. **Other Agencies**—including public agencies (code enforcement, social services, public health, etc.) and non-profit agencies, ranging from Boys & Girls Clubs to volunteer and charitable groups.

6. **The Media**—both electronic and print media.

Basic Definitions

In this media age, even the most complex issues risk being reduced to a 10-second sound bite on the evening news. The reality, of course, is that community policing is far too important and far-reaching a concept to fit into the format of "25 words or less." Yet a failure to provide simple and concise definitions risks having others (who do not understand the concept) write them for you. The following is **an expanded definition of community policing:**

> Community policing is a philosophy and an organizational strategy that promotes a new partnership between people and their police. It is based on the premise that both the police and the community must work together to identify, prioritize, and solve contemporary problems such as crime, drugs, fear of crime, social and physical disorder, and overall neighborhood decay, with the goal of improving the overall quality of life in the area.
>
> Community policing requires a department-wide commitment from everyone, civilian and sworn, to the community policing philosophy. It also challenges all personnel to find ways to express this new philosophy in their jobs, thereby bal-

ancing the need to maintain an immediate and effective police response to individual crime incidents and emergencies with the goal of exploring new proactive initiatives aimed at solving problems before they occur or escalate.

Community policing also rests on establishing community policing officers as decentralized "mini-chiefs" in permanent beats, where they enjoy the freedom and autonomy to operate as community-based problem solvers who work directly with the community—making their neighborhoods better and safer places in which to live and work.

A Concise Definition: The Nine P's of Community Policing

Community policing is a **philosophy** of full service **personalized policing,** where the same officer **patrols** and works in the same area on a **permanent** basis, from a decentralized **place,** working in a **proactive partnership** with citizens to identify and solve **problems.**

Philosophy. The community policing philosophy rests on the belief that contemporary challenges require the police to provide full-service policing, proactive and reactive, by involving the community directly as partners in the process of identifying, prioritizing, and solving problems including crime, fear of crime, illicit drugs, social and physical disorder, and neighborhood decay. A department-wide commitment implies changes in policies and procedures.

Personalized. By providing the community its own community policing officer, community policing breaks down the anonymity on both sides—community policing officers and community residents know each other on a first-name basis.

Policing. Community policing maintains a strong law enforcement focus; community policing officers answer calls and make arrests like any other officer, but they also focus on proactive problem solving.

Patrols. Community policing officers work and patrol their communities, but the goal is to free them from the isolation of the patrol car, often by having them walk the beat or rely on other modes of transportation, such as bicycles, scooters, or horses.

Permanent. Community policing requires assigning community policing officers permanently to defined beats, so that they have the time, opportunity, and continuity to develop the new partnership. Permanence means that community policing officers should not be rotated in and out of their beats, and they should not be used as "fill-ins" for absences and vacations of other personnel.

Place. All jurisdictions, no matter how large, ultimately break down into distinct neighborhoods. Community policing decentralizes police officers, often including investigators, so that community policing officers can benefit from "owning" their neighborhood beats in which they can act as a "mini-chief," tailoring the response to the needs and resources of the beat area. Moreover, community policing decentralizes decisionmaking, not only by allowing community policing officers the autonomy and freedom to act, but also by empowering all officers to participate in community-based problem solving.

Proactive. As part of providing full-service policing, community policing balances reactive responses to crime incidents and emergencies with a proactive focus on preventing problems before they occur or escalate.

Partnership. Community policing encourages a new partnership between people and their police, which rests on mutual respect, civility, and support.

Problem Solving. Community policing redefines the mission of the police to focus on solving problems, so that success or failure depends on qualitative outcomes (problems solved) rather than just on quantitative results (arrests made, citations issued—so-called "numbers policing"). Both quantitative and qualitative measures are necessary.

The Ten Principles of Community Policing

These ten principles should inform all policies, procedures, and practices associated with community policing. Many groups use them as a guide when writing their plans, referring to specific principles as justification for or explanation of certain decisions or actions.

1. **Philosophy and Organizational Strategy.** Community policing is both a philosophy (a way of thinking) and an organizational strategy (a way to carry out the philosophy) that allows the police and the community to work closely together in new ways to solve the problems of crime, illicit drugs, fear of crime, physical and social disorder (from graffiti to addiction), neighborhood decay, and the overall quality of life in the community. The philosophy rests on the belief that people deserve input into the police process, in exchange for their participation and support. It also rests on the belief that solutions to today's community problems demand freeing both people and the police to explore creative, new ways to address neighborhood concerns beyond a narrow focus on individual crime incidents.

2. **Commitment to Community Empowerment.** Community policing's organizational strategy first demands that everyone in the police department, including both civilian and sworn personnel, must investigate ways to translate the philosophy of power-sharing into practice. This demands making a subtle but sophisticated shift so that everyone in the department understands the need to focus on solving community problems in creative, new ways that can include challenging and enlightening people in the process of policing themselves. Community policing implies a shift within the department that grants greater autonomy (freedom to make decisions) to line officers, which also implies enhanced respect for their judgment as police professionals. Within the community, citizens must share in the rights and responsibilities implicit in identifying, prioritizing, and solving problems, as full-fledged partners with the police.

3. **Decentralized and Personalized Policing.** To implement true community policing, police departments must also create and develop a new breed of line officer who acts as a direct link between the police and the people in the community. As the department's community outreach specialists, community policing officers must be freed from the isolation of the patrol car and the demands of the police radio so that they can maintain daily, direct, face-to-face contact with the people they serve in a clearly defined beat area. Ultimately, all officers should practice the community policing approach.

4. **Immediate and Long-Term Proactive Problem Solving.** The community policing officer's broad role demands continuous, sustained contact with the law-abiding people in the community, so that together they can explore creative new solutions to local concerns, with private citizens serving as supporters and as volunteers. As law enforcement officers, community policing officers respond to calls for service and make arrests, but they also go beyond this narrow focus to develop and monitor broad-based, long-term initiatives that can involve all elements of the community in efforts to improve the overall quality of life. As the community's ombudsman, the community policing officer also acts as a link to other public and private agencies that can help in a given situation.

5. **Ethics, Legality, Responsibility, and Trust.** Community policing implies a new contract between the police and the citizens they serve, one that offers hope of overcoming widespread apathy while restraining any impulse of vigilantism. This new relationship, based on mutual trust and respect, also suggests that the police can serve as a catalyst, challenging people to accept their share of the responsibility for the overall quality of life in the community. Community policing means that citizens will be asked to handle more of their minor concerns themselves, but, in exchange, this will free police to work with people on developing immediate as well as long-term solutions for community concerns in ways that encourage mutual accountability and respect.

6. **Expanding the Police Mandate.** Community policing adds a vital, proactive element to the traditional reactive role of the police, resulting in full-spectrum police service. As the only agency of social control open 24 hours a day, seven days a week, the police must maintain the ability to respond immediately to crises and crime incidents, but community policing broadens the police role so that they can make a greater impact on making changes today that hold the promise of making communities safer and more attractive places to live tomorrow.

7. **Helping Those with Special Needs.** Community policing stresses exploring new ways to protect and enhance the lives of those who are most vulnerable—juveniles, the elderly, minorities, the poor, the disabled, the homeless. It both assimilates and broadens the scope of previous outreach efforts such as crime prevention and police-community relations.

8. **Grass-Roots Creativity and Support.** Community policing promotes the judicious use of technology, but it also rests on the belief that nothing surpasses what dedicated human beings, talking and working together, can achieve. It invests trust in those who are on the front lines together on the street, relying on their combined judgment, wisdom, and experience to fashion creative new approaches to contemporary community concerns.

9. **Internal Change.** Community policing must be a fully integrated approach that involves everyone in the department, with community policing officers serving as generalists who bridge the gap between the police and the people they serve. The community policing approach plays a crucial role internally by providing information about and awareness of the community and its problems, and by enlisting broad-based community support for the department's overall objectives. Once community policing is accepted as the long-term strategy, all officers should practice it. This could take as long as ten to fifteen years.

10. **Building for the Future.** Community policing provides decentralized, personalized police service to the community. It recognizes that the police cannot impose order on the community from the outside, but that people must be encouraged to think of the police as a resource that they can use in helping to solve contemporary community concerns. It is not a tactic to be applied and then abandoned, but a new philosophy and organizational strategy that provides the flexibility to meet local needs and priorities as they change over time.

What Community Policing is <u>Not</u>

To understand what community policing is also requires knowing what it is not.

*   **Community policing is not a tactic, technique, or program.** Community policing is not a limited effort to be tried and then withdrawn but instead is a new way of delivering police service to the community.

*   **Community policing is not public relations.** Improved relations with the community is a welcome by-product of delivering this new form of decentralized and personalized service to the community, rather than its primary goal, as is the case with a public relations effort. Unlike police-community relations personnel, community policing officers are held directly accountable by the community.

*   **Community policing is not anti-technology.** Community policing can benefit from new technologies, such as computerized call-management systems, if they provide line officers more free patrol time to engage in community-based problem solving. Moreover, community policing officers often benefit from access to computer terminals, cellular phones, telephone answering machines, fax machines, and other technological advancements.

*   **Community policing is not "soft" on crime.** Community policing officers answer calls and make arrests like any other line officers, but, in addition,

they involve the community in short-term and long-term proactive initiatives designed to reduce problems in the future. The distinction is that community policing considers arrest as an important tool in solving problems, not as the primary yardstick of success or failure.

- **Community policing is not flamboyant.** Dramatic, SWAT-team actions make headlines, but community policing complements such efforts by tackling chronic problems that require long-term community-based problem solving.

- **Community policing is not paternalistic.** Community policing shifts the role of the police from the "expert" with all the answers to a "partner" in an effort to make the community a better and safer place in which to live and work.

- **Community policing is not an independent entity within the police department.** While community policing officers are often the most visible symbol of the new commitment to community policing, these officers must be part of an overall strategy to form a new partnership with the community. The goal is also to make community policing officers a resource that others within the department use for information and intelligence about their beats.

- **Community policing is not cosmetic.** Community policing deals with real problems: serious crime, illicit drugs, fear of crime. It does so by addressing the entire range of dynamics that allow such problems to fester and grow.

- **Community policing is not a top-down approach.** Community policing shifts more power, authority, and responsibility to the line level by requiring that everyone in the department find ways to express the philosophy in their jobs. Community policing officers in particular must be given the freedom and autonomy to operate as "mini-chiefs" in their beats.

- **Community policing is not just another name for social work.** Helping to solve people's problems has always been an integral part of police discretion, informally if not formally. Community policing merely formalizes and promotes community-based problem solving, while maintaining a strong law enforcement component.

- **Community policing is not elitist.** The goal is to ensure that the police do not stand apart from the community, but that they become a part of the community. Community policing requires the support and/or direct participation of all of the Big Six, with average citizens playing an equal role.

- **Community policing is not designed to favor the rich and powerful.** Some have argued that community policing extends the same courteous, respectful, responsive, and caring police service that the rich and powerful enjoy to other social classes. However, community policing also implies empowering the disadvantaged, thereby providing them greater clout in securing their fair share of a variety of public services.

- **Community policing is not "safe."** By challenging the status quo and encouraging risk-taking, community policing implicitly includes allowing for failure and embarrassing mistakes.

- **Community policing is not a quick-fix or panacea.** While creative, community-based problem solving can yield immediate successes, community policing also invests in longer-term strategies designed to solve problems and improve the overall quality of life over time. Especially because of its emphasis on positive intervention with juveniles, the full extent of community policing's impact on the community may take years to become fully evident.

- **Community policing is not just another name for other police initiatives such as crime prevention, police-community relations, or problem-solving/problem-oriented policing.**

   Crime Prevention. Crime prevention is compatible with community policing—and many departments use their crime prevention officers as resource personnel for community policing initiatives—but there are differences in both their structure and their intent. Crime prevention officers are staff specialists whose duties include disseminating information on preventing crime. Community policing instead requires line-level personnel to engage in community-based problem solving that includes a strong focus on preventing crime, but which also addresses a host of the problems that can otherwise contribute to perpetuating an environment conducive to crime.

   Police-Community Relations. As noted above, community policing improves relations between the police and the community, particularly minorities, as a by-product of delivering this new form of decentralized and personalized service, whereas police-community relations focuses exclusively on the goal of improving relations with the public. As is the case with crime prevention, police-community relations relies on staff specialists, and their duties usually concentrate on networking with formal leaders of communities. The philosophy of community policing instead asks line officers to express sensitivity and attention to citizens' concerns as part of delivering a full range of police services, and community policing's organizational strategy allows officers to be held directly accountable for their behavior by the people in their beats. See Appendix A for a detailed comparison of community policing to police-community relations.

   Problem-Solving/Problem-Oriented Policing. Community policing and problem-solving/problem-oriented policing are often used interchangeably, but there are differences and distinctions. Community policing always involves using creative problem-solving techniques to address a broad range of community concerns. In contrast, problem-solving/problem-oriented policing does not always require involving the community in all aspects of the problem-solving process. Indeed, a concern with some approaches to problem-solving/problem-oriented policing is that it is applied in ways that maintain the police as the "experts," without the requirement that the community be allowed input in the process of identifying, prioritizing, and solving problems on a long-term basis. In addition, the problem-solving officers often do not work out of a decentralized office, have a permanent presence in the neighborhoods, or survey residents on an ongoing basis to determine if the problems have been solved on the long term.

As the foregoing attests, community policing has precise meanings, and just because there is police problem solving in the community, this does not necessarily mean that it meets the criteria for community policing.

The Theoretical Basis for Community Policing

The question often arises whether community policing is based on accepted theory. Recent research (Trojanowicz, S., 1992) proposes that community policing is based on two social science theories: normative sponsorship theory and critical social theory.

Normative Sponsorship Theory. Normative sponsorship theory postulates that most people are of good will and that they will cooperate with others to facilitate the building of consensus (Sower, 1957). The more that various groups share common values, beliefs, and goals, the more likely it is that they will agree on common goals when they interact together for the purpose of improving their neighborhoods.

Critical Social Theory. Critical social theory focuses on how and why people coalesce to correct and overcome the socioeconomic and political obstacles that prevent them from having their needs met (Fay, 1984). The three core ideas of critical social theory are:

> *Enlightenment.* People must become educated about their circumstances before they can lobby for change.

> *Empowerment.* People must take action to improve their condition.

> *Emancipation.* People can achieve liberation through reflection and social action.

Section Three will elaborate on these two theories and connect them to practical application.

Community Policing: A Background

Early Foot Patrol Experiments

Community policing's contemporary roots extend back to the foot patrol experiments that began in Flint, Michigan and Newark, New Jersey in the late 1970s. In both cases, research showed that not only did people in areas with foot patrol officers feel better about the police, but they also felt safer—even when, as was the case in Newark, there was no statistically significant reduction in crimes likely to be influenced by a foot patrol approach. (Flint did show a significant reduction in target crimes.)

As the researchers pondered these results, they noted that Newark had employed "undirected" foot patrol, whereas in Flint, foot patrol officers received training in how to enlist the community in creative problem solving, and the officers were given extraordinary latitude in exploring new ways to address a host of issues beyond a narrow focus on individual crime incidents.

Was foot patrol merely a "feel-good" effort that made people feel safer even if they were not demonstrably safer than before? Or did the comparison between Flint and Newark suggest that Flint's "directed" foot patrol in particular had merit beyond providing reassurance of a visible deterrent to crime?

During the early years there were a number of experiments that attempted to replicate elements of the Flint and Newark experiments. While initial results on crime reduction were mixed, pre-implementation and post-implementation surveys regularly showed a reduction in fear of crime, reduction in disorder, enhanced perceptions of personal safety, and improved relations between police and the community—particularly in minority neighborhoods. Officer perceptions of improved safety and increased job satisfaction also occurred.

A Growing Trend. As a result, more police departments were willing to experiment with what would come to be called community policing. Community policing picked up steam as it moved toward being adopted as a comprehensive new way of delivering police services. In the early years, the focus was on encouraging departments to establish community policing officers in beats, allowing them the opportunity to show what they could achieve. As anecdotal and research evidence confirmed the contribution that community policing officers were making, the focus shifted to finding ways to confront two emerging problems: external and internal backlash.

External Backlash. Community policing has periodically come under fire from the business community and from middle-income and upper-income taxpayers, especially in jurisdictions where community policing officers service only high-crime neighborhoods, and particularly if deploying community policing officers necessitated cutting the level of service that the broader community previously enjoyed. Departments faced with the challenge of finding the resources to deploy new community policing officers often cut costs by:

- instituting a slower response on non-emergency calls
- reducing or eliminating patrols in business districts
- reducing, eliminating, or assimilating special units, such as crime prevention and police-community relations
- charging for services that were previously free (such as security for parades and special events, and repeat calls due to false burglar alarms)
- taking more crime reports by phone
- asking people involved in "fender-benders" to go to the station to make a report rather than sending an officer to the scene
- eliminating "niceties" such as retrieving keys locked in cars and checking the homes of vacationers

Some citizens in the community may resent such changes. Consider, for example, the owners of small businesses who find that foot patrol officers who patrolled in front of their stores have been reassigned as community policing officers in high-crime residentials neighborhoods. Or the parent that returns home after work to find her child's bicycle stolen, but learns that policy changes to free up resources for community policing officers now mean that it may be hours (or even days) before an officer will stop by.

Time and again, departments that adopt community policing piecemeal find themselves called by those who think of themselves as "solid citizens," those who rarely, if ever, call police for help, to explain why they are being asked to pay more in taxes for less in service. Again, if community policing officers are primarily assigned to high-crime, low-income, often minority neighborhoods—where police often spend a disproportionate amount of their time—more affluent groups may begin to feel that the police are not serving their needs.

Internal Backlash. Even in those early days of the Flint experiment, internal friction was a serious problem, particularly backlash from motor officers. Some of the resistance stems from the normal reluctance of any organization to change. But much of the backlash stems from the perception that community policing implies a total rejection of the status quo—that community policing is an insult and a threat to police officers who see themselves as the "thin blue line" protecting "us" from "them." For those who view the job as answering calls, making arrests, issuing citations, and following orders, a shift to community policing can be perceived as changing the rules in the middle of the game—that they are being asked to do a job far different than the one they joined the force to perform. Community policing does not totally reject the past but attempts to build upon it. Community policing recognizes that the vast majority of officers have performed admirably in their traditional roles.

Turnover among police chiefs also contributes to internal backlash, since veterans who have "outlived" three and four chiefs during their career may feel that they can "wait out" a community policing chief who asks them to change. As one sergeant has commented, echoing many of his peers, "I've seen chiefs come and go. Why should I buy into community policing when the chief could be gone tomorrow?"

Unfortunately, the sergeant is right. During the past decade, the average tenure of police chiefs in major jurisdictions dropped from 5.5 years to between 3.5 and 4.5 years. And noted community policing chiefs, such as Drew Diamond in Tulsa and Betsy Watson, who took over for Lee Brown as chief in Houston, have been forced from their jobs.

The Ideal versus the Achievable

The community policing movement has grown beyond the stage where community policing officers must prove their worth. The challenge now is to focus on:

- developing a city-wide (jurisdiction-wide) community policing strategy, which addresses the problem of external backlash, and

- institutionalizing a department-wide commitment to community policing, which addresses the problem of internal backlash.

A City-Wide Strategy

Local Conditions

Community policing must be tailored to the needs and the resources of local jurisdictions—there is simply no way to provide hard-and-fast rules that can cover all circumstances. Consider the challenge of policing Los Angeles versus that of New York City. Though both are major cities, New York has a ratio of 5 police officers for each 1,000 residents, while Los Angeles has only 1.9. New York is so densely populated and vertical a city that if all residents of the borough of Manhattan attempted to go down to street level at the same time, there would not be enough room for them to stand, while Los Angeles sprawls across hundreds of square miles.

The image of crime in New York City may be the vicious attack of a Central Park jogger or the murders of Jusuf Hawkins and Yankel Rosenbaum, while the image of crime in Los Angeles is dominated by the 1992 riot, including the beating of Reginald Denny, and the drive-by shootings committed by some of the estimated 130,000 gang members in the city. Both cities have suffered economic reverses and both are struggling to deal with diversity, but each has its own culture and personality, its own problems, it own politics, and its own unique police tradition.

As this suggests, the specifics of a plan to implement community policing in New York should look quite different from those of a plan for Los Angeles. And community policing must adapt even more, to meet the needs of smaller cities, as well as suburban and rural areas, served by vastly different kinds of police agencies, each with its own pluses and minuses.

Yet it is possible to identify basic elements of a city-wide (jurisdiction-wide) community policing strategy, regardless of local conditions. The challenge is to adopt a strategy that ensures that everyone's needs are met with care and concern, and that requires adopting a strategy that empowers line-level personnel so that they can become effective community-based problem solvers.

Empowering Line-Level Personnel

As seen with Social Security, government initiatives that guarantee universal coverage, regardless of need, enjoy the broadest popular support. So the community policing ideal would, of course, require dividing the entire jurisdiction into manageably-sized beats, providing each beat with its own enthusiastic and trained community policing officers.

There is the question of whether all neighborhoods require the same intensity of policing. Many suburban areas are so-called "bedroom communities" that may be virtually deserted during the day, when the adults are at work and the kids are in school. Then there are upscale, walled enclaves with their own private security.

Tackling the dilemma of deployment with limited resources has been a continual problem and typically requires prioritizing beats that will be assigned police officers on an intense basis because of the severity and frequency of crime. Yet, considering the potential for external backlash, the challenge requires finding a way to deliver superior service, even to those who may not have the same intensity of police involvement. They need to be enlightened that patience with slower response for a nonlife-threatening call may pay off in the long run with less serious crime jurisdiction-wide—serious crime that often spills over into their neighborhoods.

If we return to the example of a parent who is unhappy that an officer would not come rushing because of the theft of a bicycle, the parent needs to be persuaded that effectiveness matters more than speed. This might require training the dispatcher to explain why speed is less important than a problem-solving process that offers more hope of long-term resolution.

Perhaps the process then requires that a civilian volunteer call back two or three days later to see whether the bicycle has turned up. If it has not, an officer assigned to that district or sector could stop during his or her free patrol time, and the officer could be armed with a computer printout of other reports from the area. The officer could then work with the family on organizing a Neighborhood Watch. Or the solution might require asking parents to work with school officials on targeting students who skip school, so that these truants cannot spend unsupervised afternoon hours stealing bikes.

Just as in high-crime areas, the officer challenges the family to become involved in developing solutions and sharing information. As long as the police department demonstrates care and concern for the family's problems, they are not likely to resent the fact that community policing officers are spending more time in neighborhoods where residents routinely face problems far more serious than a stolen bike.

Departments that implement a city-wide strategy of community policing can provide everyone better service than when line-level personnel did little more than dash from call to call, often to little effect.

> **NOTE:** Ideally, in the future, *all* officers should be community policing officers—not just a few designated as community policing officers.

A Department-Wide Commitment

Achieving Critical Mass

Some police departments cope with the danger of internal backlash by implementing community policing slowly, in phases. Others attempt (in vain) to evade the potential for internal resistance by adopting community policing as a limited and isolated program, placing community policing officers only in high-crime neighborhoods.

The general rule of thumb with reform movements is that at least one of every four workers must embrace the new approach if it is to have any substantive and long-lasting impact on an institution as a whole. Therefore, if community policing is applied merely as a program—deploying community policing officers in high-crime neighborhoods or placing D.A.R.E. officers in schools—it cannot reach the "critical mass" necessary to establish real reform. While such efforts are an important first step, they can never be enough on their own.

As the bicycle example demonstrates, a city-wide strategy requires a department-wide commitment, which means that all personnel must express the community policing philosophy in their jobs. All sworn and non-sworn personnel and volunteers must be trained in the community policing philosophy and in community-based problem solving. Community policing also changes the role of police managers from controllers to facilitators, whose job becomes providing the line-level personnel who deliver direct service to the community with the tools and the institutional support that they need to do their best job.

Specifics for Motor Patrol Officers

While a department-wide commitment ideally requires the support and direct participation of everyone in the department, it is crucial to instill the philosophy and practice of community policing in motor patrol officers at the outset, before all officers in the department are trained as community policing officers. Expectations for motor patrol officers should focus on three areas:

Community-Based Problem Solving. Motor patrol officers should be evaluated on and rewarded for spending their free patrol time on community-based problem solving in their districts/sectors/beats. As future sections will detail, this requires far more than just getting out of the patrol car to greet people on the street.

Support for Community Policing Officers. Motor patrol officers must be required to support community policing officers and cooperate with their efforts. Stated another way, police managers must make it clear that they will not tolerate any effort to undermine or sabotage this reform—particularly by disparaging the efforts of community policing officers in the interim before all officers become community policing officers.

"Zero Tolerance" of Excessive Force, Abuse of Authority, Incivility, Discourtesy, and/or Insensitivity. Any "bad apples" who persist in unprofessional behavior, such as hurling racial slurs or immediately resorting to unnecessary physical or verbal tactics, can undo everything that community policing hopes to achieve. Therefore, police managers must strictly enforce codes of behavior, but this also places a new responsibility on line officers to "police" their own by openly challenging any peer who begins to stray across the line.

A New Vision

Community policing does imply a profound change from the past, but it is a mistake to construe this as a total rejection of the traditional police mission. Community policing builds on the basic virtues of traditional policing by its strong support for basic policing mandates, such as rapid response to emergency calls, enforcement of prevailing laws, and promoting public safety.

Community policing proposes that it is time to move beyond working harder and faster toward working smarter through long-term, community-based problem solving. In essence, community policing assimilates traditional policing's commitment to maintaining its readiness to put out the fires whenever and wherever they erupt, but it adds to that task the goal of focusing equal effort on preventing fires.

Community policing recognizes that the police alone cannot do the job, especially now that the job demanded of them requires trying to reverse the upward spiral of violence and drugs that threatens to explode into communities that previously viewed themselves as immune. The police must not only seek the support but also the participation of the entire community, and that requires a department-wide commitment and a city-wide strategy, so that no one is ignored in building this new partnership between people and their police.

Conclusion

This section has set the tone for the rest of the book. The first two sections of the book provide general background information while the remaining sections provide more specific guidelines in the process of the long-term institutionalization of community policing.

Questions and Answers

Community policing has been called a philosophy and a strategy, a program, a tactic. Which is it? Community policing is both a philosophy and an organizational strategy—a new mission for the police, requiring new policies and procedures to attain those new goals. While the organizational strategy relies in large measure on assigning community policing officers permanently to specific beats, the philosophy and the dedication to community-based problem solving must be embraced and expressed by everyone in the department, civilian and sworn. Programs come and go. Tactics are applied, then withdrawn once the problem is solved. But community policing changes how police deliver service to the community, by encouraging a partnership between people and their police based on mutual respect and cooperation.

Was there ever a time when there was not some form of community policing? Community policing has often existed in some form in smaller communities because of the close, interpersonal relationships that exist among the residents. In small towns, officers and citizens often know each other, and they often work together to solve problems. In many ways, community policing formalizes the informal community-based problem solving that has long been the hallmark of small-town policing.

Is community policing unique to the United States? Community policing is flourishing worldwide. The National Center for Community Policing routinely fields requests for information from around the world, and there is much to be gained from cross-fertilization[1] with countries such as Great Britain and Japan.

Community policing reinvents foot patrol, with the old-fashioned beat cop as today's community-based problem solver, but if foot patrol was so effective, why did it die? Foot patrol virtually disappeared by the 1950s because of advancements in technology, with increased use of the patrol car and the police radio, and concerns that a close relationship with the community fostered corruption. Community policing does not reject technological advancement, but it suggests that nothing can outperform what committed people can accomplish working together. Concerning corruption, there is no research on whether community policing officers are more or less prone to corruption, but anecdotal evidence suggests that community policing officers may be less able to engage in undetected corruption because the community acts as an additional check on their behavior. Experience also suggests that corruption appears to be most common among officers who are not known to the community, such as undercover officers and those who remain anonymous in the community.

Since community policing emerged from foot patrol, is it just a nostalgic attempt to return to the past? While community policing shares some similarities with the foot patrol of the past, there are major differences between yesterday's beat cop and today's community policing officer. In the past, foot patrol officers were viewed as a visible deterrent to crime, and their community involvement and community-based problem-solving efforts were often conducted unofficially. Community policing formalizes and expands those roles for all line officers, with community policing officers acting as full-fledged law enforcement officers who also act as community organizers, problem solvers, protectors, and liaison/ombudsmen to other public and private agencies.

Are there any "model" community policing departments that have demonstrated that this approach is effective and viable over time? Community policing has demonstrated its effectiveness in numerous locations. However, crime rates are often used as the measure of success, which makes it difficult to judge community policing efforts. Relying on crime rates as the sole determinant of community policing's success or failure is problematic because only one out of three of all crimes (and only two of five violent crimes) is ever reported to police. In fact, as the relationship between people and their police improves with community policing, people may tell police about more crimes that would have gone unreported before. Also, the lack of job security for the chief is a serious problem in judging a particular department's efforts over time, since many impressive community policing initiatives have been dismantled by an incoming chief whose philosophy differs from that of his or her predecessor.

How long does it take for a police department to make the transition to community policing? Fully institutionalizing community policing may well require 10 to 15 years. While that sounds forbidding, the reality is that most departments can usually make the initial transition to community policing within a few months, but institutionalizing the approach to the degree that it cannot disappear takes years. For one thing, police must modify policies and procedures related to a variety of issues, such as recruiting, training, performance evaluations, and promotions. It also takes time for the culture within the department to change to a focus on community-based policing, not only because all change generates resistance, but in particular because many existing personnel chose policing because of a sincere commitment to the goals, objectives, and strategies of traditional policing. It can also take many years for community policing's proactive focus, especially its focus on the young, to demonstrate the virtues of this new way of delivering police service to the community. In addition, all of the Big Six need to make substantive changes and contributions in order for community policing to become a reality.

What is a tangible benefit of establishing this new relationship with the community? Community policing reduces and even eliminates anonymity on *both* sides. It reduces the likelihood that officers will abuse their authority or use excessive force, not only because they may be less likely to abuse people they know but also because community policing officers know that they will be back in the community the next day, where they can be held directly accountable for their actions. The residents cannot be anonymous either. They need to "step forward" and do their part.

Do community policing officers feel safer? Community policing officers can turn to residents for personal protection. Experience shows that community policing officers alone on foot often feel safer than two motor patrol officers together in a patrol car, no doubt because they have good reason to expect that the relationship with the community means that residents will be willing to come to their aid if they are threatened.

Are community policing officers specialists? In terms of role definition, community policing officers are generalists, not specialists. In addition to the skills traditionally associated with police work, the job of community policing officer also requires enhanced interpersonal and communication skills, as well as problem-solving skills. It should be noted, however, that some police unions consider the job of community policing officer as a specialty.

What is the difference between problem-oriented policing and community policing? All community policing involves problem solving, but not all problem-oriented policing is community policing. Problem-oriented policing does not always include permanent assignment of the officers, the officers working from a decentralized station, and the officers soliciting input from citizens regarding their ideas about the problems and how to solve them. Some problem-oriented policing may be an unintentional "we know what's best for you" orientation. Also, problem-oriented policing does not necessarily involve long-term evaluation to ensure that the solutions to the problems are long lasting.

Is problem-oriented policing more palatable to police administrators than community policing? The hallmark of community policing is the police and citizens working together in a partnership. That partnership can only be enhanced if there is a bond of trust. That bond is a reality when the citizens feel the government is sincere about their effort. The best way to show that it is a serious endeavor is to ask people for their opinions and concerns and then follow through with positive action. This takes a deep commitment. Some administrators and others of the Big Six do not have the commitment. Therefore, problem-oriented policing—which identifies a problem, helps solve it, and then moves on to another problem—is much more palatable to some administrators than involvement in a long-term governmental and organizational commitment.

Can community policing be counterproductive and increase the hostility of citizens rather than reduce hostility? Community policing is based on the premise that the police and the citizens together can both identify and effectively solve community problems. If community policing is just a "buzz" word and not a long-term commitment, then the escalated expectations that it creates will ultimately be its undoing. Citizens will be enticed to expect change but will be disappointed it if is not forthcoming, leading to increased resentment because the promises have not been fulfilled. Short-term appeasement is not true community policing.

How can police departments that embrace community policing avoid having "two" departments, with some of the officers community policing officers and the rest traditional officers? Ultimately, all personnel in the department should embrace the community policing philosophy but it is difficult, if not impossible, to transform the department "overnight." As much as possible police managers should try to build teamwork and not foster the "two-department" orientation. The community policing officers should not be given so many special privileges that they are considered "prima donnas." They should handle all kinds of calls, work some weekends and night shifts, and continue to perform traditional activities, like making arrests. The less they are seen as different and the more they are viewed as full-service police officers the less the chance that a department will become divided. It is better for all of the officers to practice community policing half of the time than have half of the officers practice it all of the time.

There are certain words associated with community policing. For example, what does "empowerment" mean? There are several "buzz" words associated with community policing. "Empowerment" means giving people who live in the neighborhood the necessary influence to affect the services that are supposed to be provided to them. It means that the recipients of the services should have a say in how the service is provided and delivered. Empowering people is enabling them to help themselves. Citizens cannot be patronized or "fooled" into believing that they have influence when, in fact, they do not. Improving the quality of life in our neighborhoods means a long-term commitment by both the government and the citizens—and when the government reflects the wishes and needs of the citizens, then there will be true empowerment. Empowerment also refers to the line officer being given the freedom to be creative and make meaningful decisions.

---

[1] **Cross-fertilization** is a key element in the success of community policing efforts that refers to interchange or interaction—as between different ideas, cultures or categories—that is of a broadening or productive nature.

The Planning Process:
A Community Policing Approach to Change

Armed with theory and workable definitions of community policing, the next step requires putting ideas into action. Some police departments, typically those in major cities, have an entire staff devoted to short-, intermediate-, and long-term planning. Because of the inherent difficulty in instituting change among hundreds of people, big-city police departments may not risk launching any new initiative before reams of new policies and procedures have been put in place.

On the other end of that spectrum are small departments that find it difficult to eke out any time for planning. At a recent conference on community policing, the chief of East Palo Alto, California said that he expects the number of homicides that his department will handle this year will exceed the number of sworn officers under his command, which makes it difficult to do more than deal with crises.

Most departments fall somewhere between both extremes, struggling to balance the need to plan with the constraints of tight budgets, tight timetables, and inevitable emergencies. All too often the National Center for Community Policing receives a call from a harried captain, lieutenant, or even a sergeant who has "just one question." But instead of a simple query requiring a few minutes, it turns out that the caller has been ordered by the chief to implement community policing immediately, and the question is, "What do I do now?"

Community policing is such a vital, hands-on approach that it is tempting to follow the advice in the Nike ad to "just do it." But advanced planning has its virtues, not the least of which is that it allows the department to anticipate problems before they occur. Planning also provides opportunities to improve understanding, inside and outside the department, thereby reducing resistance to change. If community policing is initiated as an experiment in one small area, obviously the challenge is far less demanding than if the plan is to adopt community policing as a department-wide philosophy and a city-wide strategy. But no matter how limited or ambitious the effort, community policing is so fundamental a change that devoting time to planning could make the difference between success and failure.

Leadership from the Top

While an imperfect analogy, perhaps we should compare planning for community policing to planning for a family vacation. If the family's goal is to make sure that everyone has a good time on the trip, then the children as well as the adults must have input into the itinerary, recognizing that the adults who pay the bills have final say. Minimizing grief on the trip also requires work up front—someone must make motel reservations, take the car in for maintenance or repair, and check out the route for potential trouble spots. Faced with such tasks, many families opt for a "package tour," but even that requires some advance work to guarantee that it will meet everyone's wants and needs.

The vacation analogy reminds us that it is the chief (or the chief and local officials) who ultimately has the final say. But leadership requires much more than exercising veto power. It is the chief who should ideally lead the charge in making the transition to community policing. Keep in mind as well that the challenge is inherently different for an existing chief who enjoys the trust and respect of the entire department than it is for a new chief specifically hired to "shape up the department" or a reluctant chief pressured to make the change by forces inside or outside the department. As this implies, chiefs must expect to have their commitment to this change tested, and planning not only helps the department set goals and objectives, but devoting time to planning also verifies the depth and sincerity of the commitment from the top.

Chiefs must also expect to provide sustained leadership. It is not enough to issue a directive and leave it at that. Chiefs must also be willing to jump the chain of command on occasion, verifying that decisions made at the top are being implemented at the line level. A chief who takes the time to stop and talk with line-level personnel periodically about how the new approach is going sends a strong message that everyone in the department should take the commitment to community policing seriously. One chief regularly walks the beat for a full shift himself, so that he can hear from people on the street—and so that his officers can see that he means it when he says he is committed to this approach.

Applying Community Policing Internally

Planning for community policing requires that departments apply the principles of community policing to the planning process itself. Community policing encourages direct, face-to-face communication—and this should also be applied to the planning whenever possible, just as planning that family trip benefits from listening to everyone's ideas and considering each individual's special wants and needs. Community policing also requires tailoring ideas to the needs and the "style" of the department and the community, and this holds true for the planning process as well.

Large departments, for example, may find it impossible or unwieldy to bring many people together often, so information and feedback must be communicated through representatives and by memo. On the other hand, smaller departments may be able to bring sizeable groups together frequently. The danger in that case, however, lies in assuming that because people know each other well and see each other almost every day that there is no need for formal interaction. The reality is that informal input may not allow people to feel that their ideas are taken seriously.

Also at issue is how to structure sessions so that individuals of different ranks feel free to air their views, without fear of jeopardizing their future. A free flow of ideas requires openness, but ground rules must emphasize mutual respect and civility.

Just as buying a prepackaged tour can seem like an appealing alternative to starting from scratch, many departments wisely seek information from other departments similar in structure to their own. However, adopting another department's plans wholesale not only risks a poor fit, but it deprives the department of internal and external dialogue that fosters understanding. While there is no need to reinvent the proverbial wheel each time, plans from elsewhere should be adapted to fit your particular circumstance.

Involving the Big Six

Community policing respects input from everyone in the community, from the powerful business owner to the welfare recipient, from community leaders to the person on the street. The same politics of inclusion should dominate the planning process, and the department should avail itself of input from inside and outside the department. As noted in the first section of the book, community policing requires involving the Big Six, and this includes seeking their input wherever possible in the planning process.

The Police Department

As noted earlier, it is usually the police chief who acts as the primary "change agent"— the individual who provides the impetus for the change to community policing. But while the chief may want to confer privately with top command about the decision, the goal is to open up the process for input from inside and outside the department as soon as possible. The general rule is, when in doubt, it is better to include rather than exclude any group whose explicit or implicit support could make a difference. Within the department, this obviously means involving top command, middle management, first-line supervisors, line-level personnel, non-sworn and civilian personnel, and special units such as investigators, narcotics, vice, crime prevention, and so on, as quickly as possible after the initial decision to make the change has been made.

A word of advice based on feedback from other departments is the importance of involving two specific groups within the department that are all too often neglected: **the union or bargaining organization** and **non-sworn and civilian personnel.** In departments with a union, involving their representatives early on is crucial, since many issues related to implementing community policing require their support. Bargaining groups may well want a voice in deciding whether the position of community policing officer constitutes a new job category, and, if so, whether this should be considered as a specialist position or as part of regular patrol. Unions must also be encouraged to amend rules to allow community policing officers the flexibility that they need, particularly when it comes to changing their hours of work on short notice. A failure to reach out for their input and support at the initial stages of planning typically risks increasing the likelihood of resistance later.

The same holds true for non-sworn and civilian personnel, who often see themselves as overworked, underpaid, and underappreciated. Many perceive themselves as second-class citizens within the department. Involving them in the planning process not only recognizes their contribution, but their support is essential. Consider, for example, the importance of involving dispatchers, since they may be called upon to explain to callers that new priorities dictated by the shift to community policing will mean that a patrol car will no longer be dispatched immediately on a cold burglary call or that the department will no longer send officers to help them if they have locked their keys in the car. As you can see, what dispatchers tell callers—both in content and tone—can depend on whether they feel that they have a stake in making community policing a success.

The Community

As discussed in detail in Section Three, the department can reach out to the community for input through techniques such as surveys and meetings. While most departments recognize the importance of outreach when it comes time for implementation, all too often they ignore opportunities to involve the community in planning. Not only is the community's input valuable, but this provides yet another opportunity to begin building a new and more open relationship with the community, so that they feel their voice is heard.

Elected Civic Officials

If we return to the analogy of the family vacation, mayors, city managers, and city council ultimately play the role of the adults who pay the bill, which gives them final say. A failure to involve them early on in the planning process can be tantamount to asking for trouble—as verified by the grim joke that the chief's office today often needs to be outfitted with a revolving door.

Admittedly, some community policing chiefs counsel that it is better to implement plans quickly, before anyone recognizes how profoundly community policing can alter the power dynamics within the community. Time and again, residents in low-income, high-crime neighborhoods have become so galvanized by the experience of taking back their streets that it emboldens them to flex their political muscle in other arenas. More than one community policing chief in "hot water" with local politicians has been bailed out because community policing's popularity with various constituencies provides a new, vocal, and supportive power base that they dare not ignore.

Yet, in most circumstances, involving local officials in the planning process is preferable, since politicians seeking votes may well want to embrace community policing as yet another benefit that they are providing to their supporters. Again, the department must decide when and how to bring elected officials on board, but deciding on a plan to approach them should definitely be an issue addressed in the planning stage.

The Business Community

Experience suggests that involving the business community in the planning process can make the difference between acceptance and resistance. In the case of large corporations and major businesses, outreach can elicit support, including financial support, for various projects. Ideally, involving them in planning will foster a new, cooperative relationship between their private security personnel and the department, perhaps with community policing officers acting as the department's liaison.

Educating prominent businesses about community policing might also mean that they will encourage their employees to participate as volunteers. In some cases, they may even be willing to allow their employees to use paid company time to help.

On the other end of the spectrum are smaller businesses and "Mom & Pop" stores— and the good news is that many are extremely supportive of local initiatives. Involving them in planning can foster close working relationships, and they may later be willing to hire individuals recommended by community policing officers. Many will contribute merchandise or services for special projects, and they can be a good source for used office equipment to furnish the community policing officer's neighborhood office.

Downtown merchants can be an especially hard sell in cases where a shift to community policing requires transferring foot patrol officers from the business district to residential areas. The ideal would, of course, be to provide all areas of the jurisdiction the level of police attention that business districts often enjoy. However, the harsh financial realities of the public sector today often dictate cutting service in one area to provide better service in areas of greater need. If at all possible, the department should try to work with the business community on finding creative ways to avoid making them feel that their needs are being ignored.

Landlords also have good reason to be included, since community policing often increases property values. Indeed, one of the toughest challenges that a government can face is maintaining affordable housing. This surfaced as a particular problem during the mid- to late-1980s, when property values in many major areas skyrocketed year after year. When enthusiastic community policing officers would succeed in stabilizing dangerous neighborhoods, enhanced public safety would spark "gentrification"—the phenomenon where ravaged areas became "hot properties" as upscale renters and buyers would flood into "bargain" areas, renovating properties beyond the reach of the poor who had been living there.

On the plus side, gentrification adds value to property, enhances the tax rolls, and provides new and attractive housing opportunities. But the obvious downside is that it often results in eviction of the indigenous, low-income residents. Not only does this burden those with the fewest resources with the problems of moving, often adding to family instability and stress, but the lack of affordable housing for the poor can contribute to the growing army of homeless on the streets, creating new problems elsewhere.

Even now that the real estate boom has stalled in most areas, the government must be sensitive to their role in maintaining affordable housing for the poor. Community policing officers often work with landlords on screening tenants, in exchange for their cooperation in improving their properties. But the local government must always balance the need to upgrade substandard housing with the need to ensure that rents do not therefore rise beyond the ability of low-income residents to pay.

As these examples verify, the transition to community policing can have a profound impact on the dynamics within a community, which means that this transition can affect the bottom lines of various kinds of businesses in different ways. Considering how powerful a constituency the business community is in any jurisdiction, a planning process that ignores their concerns and their input risks spawning serious problems down the line.

Planning can still mean making tough choices, such as pulling foot patrol officers from business districts. But the all-too-common alternative of springing such decisions on unsuspecting business owners and managers, without hearing their concerns or educating them about the rationale behind the decision, risks a far greater likelihood of sustained alienation and outrage.

Other Agencies

Expanding the police mission to include community disorder and decay means that line-level officers routinely find themselves reaching out to other public and non-profit agencies for help. This can mean involving code enforcement in efforts to upgrade substandard housing or to close drug houses. It can mean asking the sanitation department for help in removing trash. In one community, it meant urging the city planner to speed up the timetable for sidewalks in low-income neighborhoods, so that the youngsters could walk to school without slogging through the mud on rainy days. In many communities, this means involving Boys and Girls Clubs, the Salvation Army, coalitions to help the homeless, food banks, and initiatives aimed at various social problems.

Addressing this issue in planning helps in anticipating problems with lines of authority, turf battles, red tape, and all the other obstacles associated with trying to deal with agencies; otherwise, line-level personnel can easily burn out trying to be all things to all people, leaving them less and less time for their law enforcement duties.

The Media

Government and the press have long had a thorny and adversarial relationship, but perhaps no agency traditionally shies away from the press more than the police. While this advice often falls on deaf ears, the department should try to develop a working relationship with local media, so that they can assist in efforts to educate the public about what community policing is and what it can mean for the community.

If nothing else, local media should be asked to help announce public meetings. Beyond that, the goal should be to identify one or more journalists whose work seems both thoughtful and responsible, and then approach them about doing a story on this great new concept called community policing—perhaps indicating how so many of their peers have missed the boat in educating the public about what this approach can achieve. Even if the reporter cannot or will not produce articles that can help to prepare the community before the change takes place, at least you may have developed a contact willing to tout successes as they occur. Keep in mind that all jobs have unique constraints, and even an enthusiastic journalist eager to do a story on this new concept may find the resulting piece cut to a few paragraphs and relegated to the back pages if other sensational news breaks the same day. The best bet is to keep trying, in the hope that coverage overall will prove positive and helpful.

Strategic Planning

A Definition

Strategic planning is the process of examining the organization's environments, internally and externally, to determine the critical factors and best alternative strategies for achieving the goals and, therefore, the mission (Grimshaw, 1990).

The Elements

Successful planning incorporates certain key elements (Hoekwater, 1990):

Audit. A diagnosis or assessment of the current health of the organization.

Needs Assessment. Organizational needs identified by stakeholders, both internal and external to the organization.

Vision. Describes the "ideal" organization in future terms.

Values. Describes the organization's beliefs and basis for action.

Mission. Describes the organization's purpose.

General Goals. Broad performance targets essential for achieving the organization's mission.

Strategic Alternatives. Describes the optional courses for reaching the respective general goals.

Operating Objectives. Describes specific and concrete targets (operations and procedures) selected to execute the selected strategies for each goal.

Implementation. Putting the plan into action.

Monitor. Evaluating the actual performance when measured against the planned performance.

Clarifying Values

A good place to start when contemplating a shift to community policing is to clarify the values that the department stands for. Strategies to achieve this can vary, depending on the size of the department and the resources available. In large departments, the chief may decide to hold a series of organized meetings or retreats where representatives from various levels of the department can get together with a professional facilitator. In smaller departments, the chief may hold an initial meeting with top command, then expand the roster to include more and more people from the department, broadening the circle of input. In some cases, such exercises have been prompted when community surveys show general unhappiness with the police. The department may want to solicit input from the groups listed above as a way to initiate dialogue.

Such exercises typically involve identifying key words that best express what the department feels are its core values—words such as service, safety, cooperation, empowerment, courtesy, respect, commitment, integrity, involvement, and so on. The goal is to have participants consider the nature of the relationship between the police department and the community, in terms of the values, goals, and objectives of both.

Critics of this approach question whether the exercise truly produces much of lasting usefulness—and, indeed, those who have been through this process often cannot recall very many specifics later. However, it should also be noted that participants often speak of the experience as intense and as extremely valuable. Feedback suggests that, done properly, it not only helps to focus thinking about the future, but it allows participants to bond together and inspires them with a renewed sense of mission.

Mission Statement

The logical outcome from values clarification exercises is a strategy to write a new mission statement for the department that captures the essence of the new relationship with the community. Reviewing examples of mission statements from departments across the country reveals that some are 20 pages and more in length, while others have been distilled down to a paragraph or two. Again, while different departments have different needs, keep in mind that the shorter the statement, the more likely that busy people will read and remember what it says.

Two samples of one-sentence mission statements are provided below, both of which prove that you need not be wordy to convey what you stand for.

> Mission Statement: "To provide quality police service to our community by promoting a safe environment through police and citizen interaction, with an emphasis on integrity, fairness, and professionalism." [Produced by the Aurora (CO) Police Department under Chief Jerry Williams.]

> Mission Statement: "To create an atmosphere of safety and security in the Tulsa community, through proper, responsive, community-based police service." [Produced by the Tulsa (OK) Police Department under Chief Drew Diamond.]

The process developed to produce the final statement offers numerous opportunities for input. Many departments choose to assign this task to a committee under the direction of the chief, with representatives from as many areas of the department as possible who have either been assigned or who volunteer to participate. The committee may want to consider various mechanisms for input from the broader community, ranging from review of citizen surveys to creating an advisory board.

Drafts of the mission statement can be disseminated for comment and review. Another option is to provide two or three versions, then ask everyone in the department to vote. The goal is to make the final statement as clear and concise as possible, so that it will capture the widest audience.

Slogans & Logos. As part of the process of becoming a community policing department, various agencies have included producing a new slogan and/or logo, with entrants from inside and outside the department. This may be an occasion to reach out to area businesses for prizes that can be offered to the winners.

Conclusion

Planning is important, but the outcome is more important than the process. To evaluate community policing efforts in your department, you can do a self-assessment. These sample questions are certainly not meant to be exhaustive, only illustrative.

Self-Assessment Questions: A Checklist

The Department as a Whole

1. Is community policing a department-wide commitment, not just a specialty unit?
2. Does the department mission statement reflect the commitment to community policing?
3. Has the department implemented a comprehensive strategy to educate the Big Six (police, citizens, civic officials, businesses, community agencies, and the media) about the benefits, trade-offs, and risks of community policing before, during, and after implementation?
4. Has the department developed a strategy for soliciting and analyzing formal and informal feedback from the community (surveys, a citizen advisory council, etc.)?
5. Is everyone in the department, including civilians, receiving special training in community policing?
6. Beyond initial training, is there follow-up training?
7. Have recruitment and selection guidelines been changed to reflect the new commitment to community policing?
8. Have performance evaluations been changed to reflect both a quantitative and qualitative assessment?
9. Have professional guidelines been changed to reflect the commitment to community policing?

Top Command

1. Has top command structured and implemented the plan discussed above to educate and involve the Big Six (police, citizens, civic officials, businesses, community agencies, and the media)?
2. Has top command communicated to everyone within the department what is expected of them with a department-wide commitment to community policing?

continued

3.   Has top command developed and implemented a deployment plan that allows officers, both community policing officers and motor patrol officers, sufficient time and opportunity to express the community policing philosophy?

4.   Has top command addressed the need to revise hiring and promotional criteria, as well as training, to reflect the department-wide commitment to community policing?

5.   Does top command clearly communicate the differences between community policing and other proactive efforts, such as crime prevention and police-community relations?

6.   Has top command developed and implemented a plan to empower front-line employees (including civilians such as clerks and dispatchers as well as line officers)?

7.   What will top command do to foster creativity and innovation?

8.   Is top command implementing community policing as a total philosophical and organizational commitment, not as a set of tactics to be applied to specific problems?

9.   Does top command communicate that community policing focuses on both short-term and long-term results?

10.   Does top command explain to others inside and outside the department that problem solving requires focusing on arrests as only one tool in achieving results?

11.   Has top command structured and implemented a training plan to provide line officers and their supervisors information on how to optimize community policing?

12.   Has top command structured and implemented a plan to reduce internal friction, particularly between community policing officers and motor patrol officers?

13.   Has top command developed and implemented a system so that supervisors and line officers document their efforts?

14.   Does top command have a strategy to handle rotation of officers and use of officers as fill-ins that does not unduly rely on interrupting the continuity of community policing officers?

15.   Does top command make periodic visits to the field to encourage line officers and to monitor performance?

16.   What has top command done to encourage two-way information flow within the department?

17.   Has top command developed and implemented a system to measure community policing's impact on crime, fear of crime, and disorder?

18.   Has top command communicated its willingness to give officers the "freedom to fail" and to tolerate well-intentioned mistakes?

19.   Has top command developed and implemented a plan to assist officers with efforts to network with public and private agencies within the community?

20.   Has top command developed and implemented a plan to facilitate teamwork and cross-fertilization between community policing officers and sworn and non-sworn personnel in other divisions?

continued

21. Has top command structured a means of promoting and monitoring coordination among community policing efforts and the activities of other divisions and units, such as vice, narcotics, motor patrol?

22. Has top command determined and provided the resources required to implement community policing?

First-Line Supervisors

1. Have first-line supervisors been involved in the planning process, and have they been allowed input?

2. Have first-line supervisors received training in community policing?

3. Have first-line supervisors been included as part of a community policing team effort?

4. Do first-line supervisors make announced and unannounced visits to the beats to provide assistance and monitor performance?

5. Have first-line supervisors taken steps to reduce red tape?

6. Have first-line supervisors communicated encouragement for innovation and a tolerance for well-intentioned mistakes?

7. Have first-line supervisors addressed how to reduce friction between community policing officers and motor patrol officers (and special units)?

8. Have first-line supervisors communicated to motor patrol officers how they can express the community policing philosophy through their jobs?

9. Have first-line supervisors found ways to express creativity and problem solving in their jobs?

Line Officers

Beat Assignments

1. Does the community policing plan clearly define beat areas?

2. Has the community had input in determining boundaries of the beat area?

3. Is the size of the beat appropriate, as reflected in analysis of the geographic size of the beat, the number of people in the area, and the number of crimes reported and calls for service?

4. Has the officer received a permanent assignment to the beat (at least 18 months)?

Role of Line Officer

1. Are officers freed from the patrol car to allow daily, face-to-face contact with the public?

2. Have line officers been delegated sufficient authority to self-initiate innovations with a minimum of red tape?

3. Are community policing officers full-service officers who make arrests?

4. Are community policing officers provided enough time to do more than answer calls for service?

continued

5. Are community policing officers allowed the continuity required to develop rapport and trust?

6. Have community policing officers been instructed to make the effort to introduce themselves to everyone within the beat?

7. Are community policing officers given the time, opportunity, and instruction to apply problem-solving techniques to address the problems of crime, drugs, fear of crime, and community disorder and decay?

8. Are community policing officers selected for superiority in communication skills, as well as for their empathy and sensitivity to ethnic, racial, sexual, religious, and cultural differences?

Line Officers' Autonomy and Attitudes

1. Are community policing officers evaluated on parameters that reflect qualitative as well as quantitative measures appropriate to assessing community policing?

2. Do community policing officers have input into their performance evaluations?

3. Do community policing officers have sufficient time to develop rapport and trust with people in the community and to generate proactive efforts?

4. Are community policing officers used unduly to fill in for shortages elsewhere in the department?

5. Do community policing officers complain of being bogged down in red tape?

6. Does departmental policy allow line officers, including community policing officers, to talk with the media about their initiatives and activities?

7. Do officers have backing from their superiors for making well-intentioned mistakes?

8. Is duty as a community policing officer meted out as punishment?

9. Does duty as a community policing officer impair or enhance promotability, or does it have no impact on chances for advancement?

10. Do community policing officers have the autonomy to initiate projects on their own?

11. Do community policing officers have the "freedom to fail"?

12. Do community policing officers have the support of:
    —top command?
    —middle management?
    —motor patrol and other units?
    —sworn and civilian personnel?
    —the police union or association?
    —local politicians?
    —the community?

continued

13. Have community policing officers themselves actively enlisted the support, participation, or cooperation of:

—the media?

—average citizens?

—citizen volunteers?

—community leaders/groups?

—other government agencies and officials?

—public social services providers (code enforcement, social services, mental health, educators, etc.)?

—non-profit agencies (such as Salvation Army and Boy Scouts and Girl Scouts)?

—the private sector agencies (ranging from small businesses to major corporations, including landlords)?

—private security?

Problem Solving and Quality of Life

1. Do community policing officers initiate proactive short-term and long-term efforts to reduce crime, drugs, fear of crime, and community disorder, including neighborhood decay?

2. Do officers tailor their response to local priorities, needs, and resources in the community?

3. Are average citizens allowed input into the process of setting local priorities?

4. Do community policing officers take into account the capacity of the courts and corrections in the development of strategies to reduce problems such as street-level drug dealing?

5. Do community policing officers balance the efforts of the narcotics unit to target the supply side of drugs with initiatives aimed at drug demand (low-level sales)?

6. Do community policing officers work with landlords on efforts to screen tenants as a means of eliminating dope houses?

7. Do community policing officers work with code enforcement to close dope houses?

8. Do community policing officers work with drug education/treatment specialists?

9. Do community policing officers target at-risk youths for special attention?

10. Do community policing officers help to develop positive activities for youths as an alternative to misbehavior?

11. Do community policing officers interact with youngsters in ways designed to promote self-esteem?

12. Do community policing officers support families in efforts to encourage youngsters to live within the law?

13. Do community policing officers take petty crime seriously?

14. Do community policing officers promote informal conflict resolution among residents?

continued

15. Do community policing officers address the needs and problems of special groups:

—women?

—the elderly?

—the disabled?

—substance abusers?

—the homeless?

—runaways?

—youth gangs?

—juveniles?

—members of various racial, ethnic, religious, or cultural groups and those of different sexual orientations?

16. Do community policing officers work with the community on prioritizing and addressing problems with social disorder (panhandling, gambling, prostitution, etc.)?

17. Do community policing officers work with the community on prioritizing and addressing problems with physical disorder and neighborhood decay, graffiti, abandoned cars and buildings, potholes in the street, trash in yards, uncollected garbage, etc.?

18. Do community policing officers work with code enforcement and landlords to upgrade properties while maintaining affordable rents?

19. Do community policing officers delegate to others as appropriate—fellow officers, other social service providers, citizen volunteers?

Ethical and Legal Concerns

1. Are community policing officers trained in and evaluated on building rapport with members of the community in ways that promote mutual respect?

2. Has the department taken specific steps to stress respect for individual civil rights?

3. Are there safeguards in place to ensure that sworn personnel do not harass or abuse rights?

4. Have steps been taken to ensure that civilian personnel express the community policing philosophy through courteous interaction with citizens?

5. Do community policing officers take steps to restrain vigilantism within their beat areas?

6. Do community policing officers know and follow the ethical and legal constraints on their behavior?

7. Does training and supervision reinforce the importance of ensuring that community policing officers do not initiate efforts that favor one group over another?

8. Do all officers express respect for racial, ethnic, religious, cultural, and sexual differences?

9. Are measures taken to ensure that community policing officers do not function as the "good cops," while the other sworn and non-sworn personnel conduct "business as usual"?

10. Are community policing officers free of political contamination?

Understanding and Involving the Community

Defining the Community

Any attempt to explain and define the community policing movement must include grappling with what the word "community" is intended to mean in this context. Though it might at first seem that a simple, one-sentence definition would suffice, community can mean very different things to different people.

Understanding the dynamics of "community" is critical to the prevention and control of crime and disorder as well as fear of crime. Social control is most effective at the individual level. Personal conscience is the key, because it can keep people from crossing the line even when no one is looking.

The family, the next most important unit affecting social control, is obviously instrumental in the initial formation of the conscience and a continued reinforcement of the values that encourage law-abiding behavior. The extended family, especially if they are in close geographic proximity, and neighbors are also important in supporting the norms of positive behavior.

Unfortunately, because of the reduction of influence exerted by neighbors, extended families, and even the family, social control is now often more dependent on external control—the criminal justice system—than on internal self-control.

There is now a distinct difference between the geographic community and a **community of interest**—a distinction easily blurred in the past when both kinds of communities typically overlapped to cover the same population. This has particular relevance to the use of "community" in community policing because crime, disorder, and fear of crime can create a community of interest within a geographic community. Enhancing and emphasizing this particular community of interest within a specific geographic area can provide the impetus for residents to work with the community policing officer to create a positive sense of community. Therefore, the use of the word "community" in community policing can refer to many, sometimes overlapping, entities. It is **community of interest,** generated by crime, disorder, and fear of crime, that allows community policing officers an entree into the geographic community. Then the officer and the residents can develop structures and tactics designed to improve the overall quality of life, allowing a renewed community spirit to build and flourish.

Technological Changes

Three major technological changes—**mass transportation, mass communication,** and **mass media**—have played a great role in the divorce between geography and the community. In the model of the past, the overlap between a community of interest and a geographic community blurred the distinction between the two. For example, when a crisis occurred—perhaps a farmer's barn burned—neighbors linked by a common geography and a community of interest pitched in to help the farmer build a new barn. While altruism may well have played a role, the underlying reality also operating was that neighbors cooperated because the farmer who lent a hand today knew he might well need a helping hand tomorrow. Such instances are not often the case today with our disjointed communities.

The effects of mass transportation and mass communication have obviously contributed to the breakdown of the geographic connection and the traditional definition of community. However, scant attention has been paid to the role the mass media plays. Instead of defining ourselves by the neighborhood communities where we live, we are likely to label ourselves in terms invented and reinforced by the mass media: baby boomers, born-again Christians, feminists, yuppies, and so on. For many in today's society, we are what we do; we define ourselves primarily in terms of career. Those who find less satisfaction in their work might define themselves by their leisure activities—as triathletes, classic car buffs, and antique hounds. Others see themselves in more political terms: pro-choicers, pro-lifers, tax-protesters, peace-activists.

When pairing community of interest with geography was still relevant in defining community, a certain political unity also was implied. That is why, in an earlier era, political candidates would make required visits to neighborhoods, particularly ethnic neighborhoods, in search of votes. Many such neighborhoods literally voted as a bloc because their shared community of interest meant that certain issues were of particular concern. Obviously, the pervasive influence of mass media has played a role in changing the political equation in community, as television ads have replaced handshaking as the most effective political tool.

The rise of technological, political, and economic changes that have so altered the definition of community have also ushered in an explosion in the rates of serious crime. Those same forces that fragmented traditional communities may well have played a crucial role in eroding the internal control that helped control crime. This is crucial to understanding the philosophy of community policing, since its underlying rationale includes the proposition that, by using crime, disorder, and fear of crime as the issues to unite the community and the police, this new partnership between people and the police can be the catalyst in restoring the traditional sense of community that has proved so effective in bolstering internal control, which has done such a good job of preventing and controlling crime in the past.

Perhaps because we have failed to study and understand the ways in which communities have changed, that all-important sense of community (which could well be the most important weapon in fighting crime) has often been lost, and even a strong external control (the criminal justice system) can never substitute for internal control. The sad fact is that many communities have lost the collective will to fight the battle against drugs, decay, disorder and crime. By getting back to the basics and by stimulating communication between the police and neighborhoods—processes that allow residents to rebuild that traditional sense of pride in community life—the community policing movement holds the promise of improving the quality of life in our cities. Perhaps even more importantly, we must recognize the need to restore our communities before this opportunity disappears forever.

Involving the Citizens*

After visiting many communities over the years, some stand out for their positive community activism, which manifests itself in fostering a partnership between the police and the residents. These communities range from Chicago, Illinois; to Newton County, Ohio; to Boston, Massachusetts; to Pasadena, California; to Lansing, Michigan; to McAllen, Texas.

Whenever citizen groups, private industry, or private citizens have attacked the problems of crime, fear, and disorder, the results have been remarkably better than those of the formal criminal justice system. Unfortunately, however, too few communities have been able to construct efforts that systematically coordinate the resources of the community with those of the formal system (see Section Five on the Neighborhood Network Center). There are so many social, political, and economic problems involved in mobilizing community resources that many communities settle for an ad hoc, piecemeal effort, to avoid tackling the problems inherent in a unified approach. Full citizen participation in community problem solving, while not new to the American scene, is certainly not currently evident in many communities. Citizen participation often has been limited to the responsibility to be informed about public issues, to vote for elective representatives, and to abide by the legal and administrative mandates of public officials. Special-interest groups have been a traditional vehicle for citizen participation, but many of the policy-making decisions take place at state and national levels. As a result, individuals may perceive their participation in local church, union, business, and political groups as unnecessary or as not yielding sufficient returns for the cost.

As mentioned earlier, one of the first problems facing anyone attempting to initiate efforts that deal with crime, disorder, and fear is the nature of the community itself. A cohesive farming community of 5,000 people, an industrial city, a capital city, a university town, a metropolis—all differ radically in terms of crime rate, types of crime, the degree of cultural homogeneity or heterogeneity, financial and organizational resources, political conditions, and fear of crime. Many neighborhoods are united by being physically isolated from the larger community, others by social class or ethnic composition. Still others are conglomerations that may not exhibit any of the features usually associated with the term "neighborhood." This means that **community of interest** is the element most likely to produce unity.

---

*The information contained in this section first appeared in two publications: *Criminology,* February 1972, "Police-Community Relations: Problem and Process," Robert C. Trojanowicz, and *Community-Based Crime Prevention,* Robert C. Trojanowicz, John M. Trojanowicz, and Forest M. Moss, Goodyear Publishing Co., 1975.

Action Steps

The difficulties involved in motivating large numbers of alienated citizens have been explored over the years. Motivation and participation are difficult to sustain over extended periods of time. Public administrators seldom use citizens efforts, which they consider uninformed and amateurish. Indeed, public officials often think that involving citizens merely provides opportunities for them to drag their feet or even to sabotage worthwhile efforts. Any new effort will also have to deal with all the problems endemic to the community, ranging from funding, to red tape, and other factors that inhibit effective problem solving. No single effort has been shown beyond a reasonable doubt to be foolproof in preventing crime, disorder, and the fear of crime. This, however, should not stop concerned persons from working together.

As mentioned earlier, two theories are relevant to community policing: **normative sponsorship theory** and **critical social theory.** Simply stated, normative sponsorship theory proposes that a community effort will only be sponsored if it is normative (within the limits of the established standards of the community) to all persons and interest groups involved. Furthermore, in an attempt to initiate community development, it is of major importance to understand how two or more interest groups can have sufficient convergence of interest or consensus on common goals to bring about program implementation. Each group involved and interested in implementation must be able to justify, and hence legitimize, the common group goal within its own pattern of attitudes, values, norms, and goals.

The more congruous the attitudes, values, norms and goals of all participating groups, the easier it is for them to agree upon common goals. The participating groups, however, do not necessarily have to justify their involvement in or acceptance of a group goal (Sower, 1957).

In other words, this theory proposes that:

- For a community to begin any new effort, the effort itself must reflect the community's basic standards.

- And for the community to come together to start this new effort, at least two of the major groups in the community must agree that the project is worth doing and that it is consistent with their attitudes, values, norms, and goals.

- In addition, the more that the groups willing to take this leadership role have in common, the more that they can agree on common goals, while recognizing that subsequent groups that sign on to help may not have the same reasons for coming on board.

The community policing officer plays a very important role in the normative sponsorship process because local leaders do not often emerge and take it upon themselves to solve community problems. It can take the officer, as community catalyst, to stimulate interest, identify leaders, and help them solve their problems. After the officer acts as catalyst, stimulus, and leader, it is interesting to note that as the community becomes aware of available resources and learns the problem-solving process (which many of us take for granted), the requests for assistance typically decrease. In other words, community policing officers, working in a designated area, can put themselves out of a job eventually, not only because the citizens do more for themselves, but because once the philosophy of community policing takes hold in the organization, all officers on all shifts will become community policing oriented and hence the need for the specially designed community policing officer will dissipate. This, however, will take many years to be fully integrated into the department.

The following are the steps necessary to initiate community action to solve problems of crime, disorder, and fear of crime.

Step 1: Information Gathering

People often talk about controlling crime, disorder, and fear without an awareness of the underlying dynamics and without any precise measures of the extent of problems in the community. Crime reporting can provide a beginning point, but it should be expanded to include an estimate of unreported crime. Crime information, both reported and unreported, can be obtained from many sources, such as a sampling of citizens, members of the medical profession, the clergy, and those who work at rape crisis centers, drug-abuse hotlines, and so on. Victimization surveys are additional sources of information. Appendix B presents an instrument for the analysis of the resources, strengths, and weaknesses of the community. Completing this document before entering into community policing will be useful in providing a base of information.

Public officials often operate in a climate of high demand and limited resources. They usually react only to blatant crises that immediately threaten public equilibrium. Yet when community groups come together to attempt to do what government cannot or will not do for them, their actions should be based on good, solid information. In other words, the collection of information is an initial step in beginning the long-term process of improving neighborhoods.

Neighborhoods and their problems differ, so the analysis of the information gathered will need to be area specific. For example, if an area of the city is experiencing a high rate of car theft, it then becomes important to know the physical characteristics of the area. Is the problem related to poor lighting? Is it an area of high transience? Is it a residential area? What is the population density? What are the cultural and economic demographics in terms of income, race, ethnicity, unemployment rates and so on?

Have any car thieves been arrested? If so, is a profile emerging? What are they doing with the stolen vehicles?

What is the current level of police patrol? How are citizens reacting to the problem? Are there any community organizations that can provide immediate resources? Can community organizations be developed? The goal is to ask as many questions as possible, to develop a clearer picture of what is going on.

Car theft is merely one example of the many serious problems that can escalate when the community feels that it has no way to fight back. The problems posed by illicit drugs are another obvious example. Yet dealing with such crises often leaves little time to explore the underlying dynamics. The police also need answers to questions such as: What are the employment opportunities for young people already headed down the wrong path? What effect can the police and the community working together have on that problem?

Most of the crime in our communities is perpetrated by young people, often youths with too much idle time and too little hope for the future. Considering the magnitude of this problem, officers should attempt to gather information related to the twin issues of juveniles and job opportunities. What is the the availability of public transportation and recreation opportunities within the area? What is the degree of citizen disapproval of or concern about the situation?

A. **Information-Gathering.** Establish a task force to determine:

1. Youth population, by area

2. Number of youths employed

3. Extent of delinquency

4. Community-wide employment opportunities and existing programs

5. Extent of job preparation training, if any, and relationship to job market

6. Extent of local, state, and federal funding for use in employment projects and the manner in which it is being used

7. Nature of nonofficial community or neighborhood resources being employed, if any

8. Specific problems experienced by youths, delinquents, probationers, or parolees relative to

a) Job placement
    (1) Prejudice against past record
    (2) Prejudicial state licensing requirements
    (3) Lack of bonding acceptability
    (4) Poor verbal skills
    (5) Unacceptable appearance
    (6) Racial discrimination
    (7) Poor performance
    (8) Prejudice against youths
    (9) Lack of occupational skills
    (10) Lack of general educational skills

b) Job retention
    (1) Poor punctuality and transportation problems
    (2) Lack of acceptance by public being served
    (3) Prejudicial attitude of other employees
    (4) Personal information or habits reflecting poorly on company
    (5) Poor adaptability to increased responsibility
    (6) Resistance to supervision or authority
    (7) Poor self-discipline
    (8) Lack of trustworthiness

c) Promotion
    (1) Inability to accept increased responsibility
    (2) Prejudice of management
    (3) Employee resistance

9. Extent of diversion within the formal criminal justice system (for example, employment training or counseling in lieu of pressing charges or formal trial)

10. Locus of responsibility for diversionary programs and basis of funding

11. Existence of diversionary programs within the community youth service bureau or the police juvenile bureau or division

12. Number of probationers or parolees within the community, expressed needs of probation and parole officers, and specific problems of the individuals they supervise (lack of suitable clothing for job interviews, lack of study areas at home, and transportation expenses, for example)

B. **Encouraging Coalitions.** Motivate community groups and citizens to create or direct resources already in existence to solve the problem by:

1. Relating the problem to the economic welfare of community safety and increasing earnings within a particular area

2. Challenging existing social, fraternal, religious, professional, and business groups to sponsor a number of youths, to prepare action alternatives, and to make staffing proposals

3. Determining potential resources and attempting to enlist business people for the purpose of advocacy

C. **Specific Tasks.**

1. Job market analysis and job development

   a) Establish a job bank
   b) Obtain commitments to hire
   c) Get endorsements from satisfied employers
   d) Ensure full use of established agencies

2. Training

   a) Develop training courses in specific needed skills in neighborhood schools, church groups, and community colleges
   b) Provide occupational counseling
   c) Make arrangements for occupational sampling
   d) Establish supportive services while in training

3. Placement

   a) Match interests and skills to job
   b) Provide supportive meetings and counseling
   c) Provide new opportunities through
      (1) Night school
      (2) Community service
      (3) Neighborhood councils
      (4) Big Brothers and Sisters

d) Do periodic follow-up

e) Recruit successful probationers, parolees, and youths as spokespersons and for training in community responsibility

This list can be extended. Since such sub-goals can be tackled by almost any interested citizen or citizens' group, they should invite community participation. The community policing officer can be the stimulus for the effort.

Step 2: Analysis of the Community

Critical social theory is the second major theory associated with community policing. This theory involves critically analyzing the problems of the community so that the citizens and community policing officers can be **enlightened,** and then **empowered,** and ultimately **emancipated** to become fully functional in working together to solve problems.

It is highly improbable that an outsider to the community could effectively organize a community to deal with crime, disorder, and fear. It would first be necessary to critically analyze and become intimately familiar with the community, its history, its process of development, its past conflicts, and its current politics and problems. All these factors influence the attitudes of the citizens and the acceptability of various problem-solving techniques. Consideration in analyzing the community should include the following:

1. Economic base
    (a) Single-industry or business center base
    (b) Expansion plans
    (c) Community attitudes toward expansion
    (d) Labor-management crisis
    (e) Present and future job market

2. Cultural aspects
    (a) Single or multicultural community
    (b) Class lines and prior conflict, if any
    (c) In multicultural community, nature of equilibrium, if any, or strife
    (d) Official response to cultural situation, in terms of favoritism, distribution of services, alignment of elected officials
    (e) Mobility patterns

3. Social organizations
    (a) Number and nature of social, fraternal, and church organizations
    (b) Conflict, cooperation, or coalition, if any, for common cause
    (c) Reactive organizations, if any
    (d) Political affiliations of organizations and attachments to particular social movements
    (e) Existing social programs and projects
    (f) Potential for creation of new organizations

4. Official functions
   (a) Punitive formal justice agencies
   (b) Nonpunitive approaches created or supported by formal agencies
   (c) History of attempts to create programs or supplement official crime prevention programs
   (d) Current coordination and planning that is fragmented or centrally assumed
   (e) Inter- and intra-agency conflict or cooperation; attitudes of formal justice and social agencies toward each other

5. Crisis handling
   (a) Natural disasters and social crises that have influenced attitude formation
   (b) Racial strife and its resolution or nonresolution
   (c) Sensational crime, by neighborhood or area; presence of organized crime, if any
   (d) Public perceptions of adequacy of officials in responding to past crises, especially regarding crime, disorder, and fear of crime.

Step 3: Relevant Group Identification

Before any community effort can take place, groups relevant to the problem-solving activity must be identified. We have discussed earlier the Big Six: the police, the community, elected civic officials, the business community, other agencies, and the media. All relevant groups should be involved so that they "buy into" the community policing effort. The community policing officer is the catalyst.

Social situations change, therefore efforts must not only be founded on a thorough analysis—there must be constant updating. Identifying the basic values of those involved is also necessary, so that when any effort is initiated it reflects their values and concerns.

Obviously, neighborhoods and communities are diverse and complex. Within the context of a *community of interest,* after information gathering and the analysis of the community, it is then necessary to begin community meetings, both city-wide and at the neighborhood level.

The city-wide meeting should be organized to discuss a proposal to launch community policing, with follow-up meetings at the neighborhood level. While some elements may not apply (for example, rural areas may not have a suitable site for a central meeting), this is offered as a general guide.

The Initial City-Wide Meeting. The initial city-wide meeting is held to:

- Educate the public about the history of community policing and how it could fit the needs of the community.

- Give the citizens the information that was gathered through the community analysis (recognizing, however, that it will be important when specific beat areas are identified that the community policing officer will continue the information-gathering process relevant to the specific beat).

- Obtain feedback from the citizens regarding what they perceive as the general problems of the jurisdiction.

- Begin to identify the factors that will be considered when initiating the specific community policing effort, such as the criteria to be used when selecting the beats.

- Formalize a tentative timetable for moving the community policing effort from the planning stage to implementation.

- Be prepared to have a tentative skeletal proposal ready for initial discussion.

Choosing a Site for the Meeting. Attention to detail can help assure that the meeting will be a success. The sponsors of the meeting, usually community activists, governmental officials, police officials or a combination of such leaders, should ask themselves the following questions before settling on the meeting site:

- Have similar meetings been called in the community from which to draw comparisons?

- What is the expected turnout?

- Is the site large enough to accommodate the expected turnout?

- Is there sufficient parking at the site?

- Is the site accessible to all of the community residents?

- Is the site accessible to public transportation?

- Will there be transportation for people who cannot afford it?

- Will the citizens be comfortable in the room if the meeting turns out to be a long one?

- Are the acoustics adequate so that everyone will be able to hear clearly?

- Is the lighting adequate?

- Does the setup accommodate input from all who attend?

Equipment. Is the equipment functioning well so that the meeting can go smoothly, without delays and disruptions? The following questions can help the sponsors determine the equipment they will need.

- Will a public address system be needed?

- If so, how does one go about securing it?

- Is it available at the site?

- How is it operated and who is in charge of it?

- Will additional microphones in the aisles be needed to hear questions from the audience?

- Is any audio/visual equipment needed?

- Who will operate it and be responsible for it?

- Are there back-up supplies or equipment on hand (spare bulb for projector, microphones, extension cords)?

Scheduling the Meeting. After determining the meeting site and identifying needs, a time and date must be chosen that will make it easy for large numbers of citizens to attend. The following are important considerations:

- *The date.* Experience dictates that a week night works best, since many people are unwilling to give up weekend days or nights.

- *The time.* Make it early enough for working people to get to bed at a reasonable time, but late enough so they can have dinner first; 7:30-8:00 works well.

- *Potential conflicts.* Be sure that the date you choose does not conflict with a holiday or important cultural or sporting event.

- *Confirming the date and time.* Be sure that whoever is in charge of scheduling the site has confirmed the date and time with the landlord.

Publicizing the Meeting. If the meeting is to be a success, there will have to be a large turnout of citizens. Get the citizens excited and talking about the meeting. Promotion cannot be overdone.

- Announce the meeting early enough so that citizens can plan ahead, but not too far in advance that the date is easy to forget.

- Prepare a press release for the media and send it to the newspapers, shopping guides, television and radio stations.

- Ask the local media to do a story on the proposal that has been presented to the citizens.

- Organize a press conference and contact all local media, as well as political leaders, business leaders, citizen leaders, and leaders from the many diverse groups that usually exist in the community.

- Take advantage of community calendars or community-service announcements in the local media.

- Utilize the social organizations of the community to spread the word; perhaps businesses, community-service groups, block clubs, neighborhood associations, hospital associations, or churches would be willing to make an announcement in a newsletter, catalog, advertisement, or in the envelope with their monthly billing (utility companies, for instance). Recruit volunteers to hang posters and distribute flyers. Have schools send an announcement home with children.

The Agenda. The discussion of crime, disorder and fear of crime—and how community policing can make a difference—is what will give the initial city-wide meeting its direction and momentum. Without it, the meeting could easily degenerate into a formless "rap" session. It is hoped that the citizens will have become familiar with the issues ahead of time and will come prepared with comments and questions. A suggested agenda is as follows:

- *Presentation of the problem (and a tentative proposal)*—in this case a proposal to develop a partnership between the Big Six, to address crime, disorder, and fear of crime problems. After the general information is presented, there should be a discussion.

- *Questions and comments by citizens.*

- *Agreement on the thrust* of the community policing effort and the *beginning of discussions* about various aspects such as criteria for selecting beats.

- *Group discussions.* Sometimes breaking the group up into small groups is effective.

- *Adjournment.*

The Neighborhood Meeting. After the initial city-wide meeting, the next step is individual neighborhood meetings. If there are community organizations (block watches and such), these can form the basis for the neighborhood meetings. Some areas of the city may not have formalized neighborhood associations or block watches, but people who live there are potentially even more fearful and concerned about disorder and crime. If there are no formal organizations, use a local school or a church—any method to get smaller groups of people at the neighborhood level together will be useful.

The goals of the neighborhood meetings will be similar to the goals of the city-wide meetings. It is a good opportunity to obtain further critiques about using community policing as a method of dealing with the problems. The citizens will have rudimentary information about community policing and may have attended the first city-wide meeting. Now they must have time to examine its appropriateness for their neighborhood. The person(s) who conducts these meetings can be from any or all of the groups mentioned earlier. It is mandatory however that at least one police official be present.

The overall goal of the neighborhood meeting is for citizens, in cooperation with the police and others of the Big Six, to discuss the appropriateness of community policing for their area, and whether there will be support for it. Other issues may be discussed, such as the criteria for being an experimental area, the beat boundaries, and options for the location of the office.

Tradeoffs that are required for community policing should also be discussed: people doing more for themselves, longer response time for nonlife-threatening calls, and the need for volunteers.

Specifically the participants may:

- Discuss ways that volunteers can be useful, like typing newsletters, writing articles, organizing fundraisers to pay for certain office equipment, making call-backs to victims of crimes, tutoring young people who are headed in the wrong direction, and so on.

- Measure community support. See how many citizens are involved in block clubs, how many volunteers are willing to work with young people, the elderly, or special groups. How many volunteers are willing to work on beautification projects? Even though this will be an ongoing process, it is helpful to get a gauge, initially, as to what the level of involvement might be.

- Begin to identify problems unique to the neighborhood, prioritize them, identify those persons who are willing to work on them, and possibly even discuss initial identification of leaders who will have a long-term commitment.

- Talk generally about the role of the community policing officers and obtain suggestions of what some of the criteria should be for evaluating officers.

There may be one or more meetings in the neighborhood. It is useful to get as much information as possible at the neighborhood meetings, so that the citizens can make a pitch at the final city-wide meetings as to why their neighborhood should be one of the first experimental areas. It is the goal that community policing will eventually be practiced in all areas of the jurisdiction.

As mentioned above, it is imperative that a police representative attend the meeting(s). This person can:

- Act as the formal representative of the department.

- Make sure that the views of the police department are known and understood.

- Offer constructive criticism relative to suggestions made by citizens and let them know if such suggestions are workable and legal.

- Act as an arbitrator or broker for disputes between people.

- Aid the process of developing a final neighborhood proposal with a basic consensus.

Note: The leader of the meeting, whether a police officer or not, should primarily facilitate and not dominate.

Final City-Wide Meeting. The final city-wide meeting is held to provide a jurisdiction-wide plan. Although there may be minor changes and amendments, the process of planning and writing a skeletal proposal has for the most part been completed. Now the community policing effort has been planned and discussed and, depending on whether the funding has been secured and needed political support has been forthcoming, the effort is ready for implementation, usually on an experimental basis. Because not all areas of the city will initially have a community policing officer, there needs to be criteria for the selection of the beats.

Identifying Beats. When making a switch to community policing, the change cannot be accomplished overnight and is usually on an experimental basis. Most likely there is not enough funding to put community policing officers in all neighborhoods. Therefore, there must be a system in place to prioritize where officers should go first—usually the areas with high crime and disorder win out over low-crime neighborhoods as the beats for community policing officers. Once the experiment is successful, it can then be expanded to other areas. Lansing, Michigan, for example, started with one beat and now has thirteen, with plans for even more. A priority list can be established so that it is usually just a matter of going down the list of areas when new beats are selected.

Criteria for Prioritizing Areas.

- Total calls for service

- Number of priority calls

- Total number of criminal offenses

- Total number of reported crimes

- Total number of Part 1 crimes

- Number of suppressible crimes

- Number of addresses in the area with five or more calls for service in the past six months

- Number and location of juvenile arrests

- Building/zoning code violation complaints

- Population density of rental properties—victimization data

- High density of rental properties—socioeconomic data

- Community resources already in place (churches, neighborhood watch, schools, parks, neighborhood organizations)

- Number of drug houses in the neighborhood

- Number of narcotic offenses in area

When the final city-wide meeting has been adjourned, it should be clear to all how community policing is generally going to operate in the jurisdiction. Specifically, everyone should know:

- Where the experimental beats are going to be and how they are going to be selected.

- What shifts the community policing officer will work, even though final determination will be made once the officer is in the particular neighborhood and sees what the problems are. In most cases the officer will work variable shifts depending on the problems in the area.

- The general duties of the community policing officer, even though they will be dependent upon the particular problems of the neighborhoods where he or she is stationed.

- Some suggestions as to where the decentralized office will be located in the community, even though the final determination will be made at the neighborhood level.

- The procedure for contacting the community policing officer.

- How the community policing officer, motor patrol and other units of the department will interact with each other. (In some cases the "regular" motor officers will be the deliverers of the community policing service, so there will not be an "experimental" community policing officer.)

- That the Big Six will begin communicating with each other.

After the final city-wide meeting, neighborhood meetings will continue—especially in those areas that will be assigned a community policing officer.

Step 4: The Identification of Leadership

Some citizens will have attended many of the neighborhood meetings, but they are not all necessarily potential community leaders. People willing to get the process started must be identified. Most persons who become actively involved in the community policing effort are not motivated so much by their own victimization or fear of crime as by a general interest in the neighborhood and community. Look for people who reflect the neighborhood's attitudes, values, norms, and goals, since they should know how best to stimulate and perpetuate citizen support.

These leaders may hold a position in the formal structure of a community organization, such as an officer in a block club, or they may hold a command rank in the police department or an administrative position in a social agency. They may not necessarily have such a formal position in either the community or a community agency, but may exert influence on community members.

Identification of the leaders is accomplished through a process of sampling members of the relevant organizations and asking such questions as:

- "Whom do you or most of the people in your organization turn to for advice on problem solving?"

- "Who in the organization is respected, has power and influence, and has a reputation for getting things done?"

After the sampling process is completed, construct a list of individuals whose names have been mentioned most often as leaders. The sampling process is important for leadership identification. Do not assume that sampling is unnecessary because leaders are already known. Leadership is not static, and those persons assumed to be leaders because of their formal or informal position are not necessarily the major source of power or influence. The identification of true leadership is mandatory if problem solving is to take place and be successful on the long term.

Regardless of the method of selection, leaders should exhibit many of the following characteristics:

- An ability to relate personally to the effort, preferably by living in the neighborhood.

- An orientation to action in solving problems as opposed to rhetoric.

- An ability to identify with the people involved and, ideally, to be recognized by that group as a natural spokesperson.

- The ability to innovate, inspire action, and stimulate continued and widespread citizen participation.

- The ability to encourage citizen response from all segments of the community.

Step 5: Bringing Leaders of Relevant Groups Together

After leaders of the relevant groups have been identified, the next step is bringing the leaders together. They should be told that they have been identified by their peers as influential leaders interested in community policing. The initial meetings (usually chaired by a community person) will be somewhat unstructured. The major objectives of these meetings will be to:

- Facilitate the expression of feeling about the apparent problem.

- Encourage relevant groups to exchange perceptions about each other. (Many agencies are suspicious of each other, and citizens may be suspicious of agencies as well.)

- Produce an atmosphere conducive to meaningful dialogue so that misperceptions can be identified and any factors contributing to the causation of the problem can be discussed.

- Identify self-interest groups, and point out how each group will benefit from cooperative problem solving to prevent crime and disorder.

It is not the purpose of the initial meetings to produce attitude changes or to develop a "love relationship" between the relevant groups. Negative attitudes will change as trust builds when they work together on program development and implementation.

Whenever diverse interest groups assemble, they will often have biased opinions, misinformation, and negative perceptions of one another. If they are defensive and have difficulty talking openly, the initial stages of the process will be hindered—and this can have unfavorable implications for future cooperation and program implementation.

Experience has shown that many groups initially make accusations about each other. The police, for example, are accused of being authoritarian and aloof, while the community is accused of complacency and lack of cooperation. Agencies often point fingers at each other. Social service workers may call the police "hard-headed disciplinarians," and the police may retaliate by calling social workers "permissive do-gooders." If the elements of truth in the accusations are not handled in an honest manner, if the factors that contributed to the perceptions are not identified, and if these perceptions are not discussed, then the communication process will be shallow and the total problem will not be understood.

No group should be allowed to monopolize the session, and no meeting should be allowed to get out of hand to the point where people become offensive or rude. The admission of the obvious truth of some of the accusations by the relevant groups will be helpful in establishing an atmosphere of trust and credibility. This will facilitate understanding and cooperation.

However, the communication process between the relevant groups should be more than merely the denial or the admission of "facts." It should include a discussion of factors that can contribute to misperceptions. For example, the citizens could be informed of the policies of the various agencies and the effect these policies have on the delivery of services to the community. Insight in this area may be helpful in explaining how certain administrative considerations must be weighed and how certain priorities are established. Citizens could also share with the agencies the reasons why they become frustrated with the apparent lack of concern and the impersonality of bureaucracies. This will facilitate agency personnel empathizing with the citizens and vice versa. Interagency misperceptions can also be neutralized through the process of sharing problem-solving approaches and reasons why an agency takes a particular orientation.

The increased empathy between relevant groups will help destroy misperceptions and provide the relevant groups with new insights into individual and organizational behavior. This will establish a basis for future understanding and cooperation.

The first few meetings are usually typified by the:

- Unstructured expression of feelings and perceptions.

- Admission of "real facts."

- Discussion of the factors contributing to misperceptions.

- Facilitation of understanding.

- Increasing the number of positive perceptions between the groups.

The sessions then begin to take a more focused and less emotional orientation. If the initial meetings have achieved their objectives, the stage is set for the next phase of the process.

Step 6: The Identification of Areas of Agreement and Disagreement

Once the perceptions of the various groups have been identified, the information can be presented, usually on a flip chart, and then discussed. The perceptions of the various groups can then be compared, and areas of agreement and disagreement can be identified and discussed. For example, the perception that the police have of their role can be compared with the perception that the community has of the police role and vice versa. This comparison can also be made with the other relevant groups—police with social service workers, social service workers with the community, and so on.

The perceived roles of the groups can also be compared with the actual behavior of the groups, and then an evaluation can be made as to whether the particular group is acting in accordance with how it should perform or how it is perceived.

As a result of comparing perceptions with behavior, it will be evident if the groups are preforming as they should be or if they are not fulfilling their expected roles. There is usually more consensus than anticipated about what the role of the groups should be. The problem usually is that each of the groups has its own unique limitations and constraints because of past history and/or economic problems.

Step 7: Implementation

After areas of agreement and disagreement have been identified, an effort can be made to incorporate the areas of agreement so that the major aspects of the initiative will be acceptable to all groups. The groups will not necessarily agree in all areas, but there will usually be enough common areas of agreement to allow cooperation.

Many groups will be both inspired and enlightened to learn how many areas of agreement exist which, at first glance, might not have been apparent. There will generally be agreement on major goals, such as the need for crime and disorder control for more positive and effective communication, and for cooperation between the groups. Areas of consensus may decrease as specific techniques for problem solving are identified and alternatives for implementation are suggested by each group. This will not be a major problem, however, because if the principles of normative sponsorship theory and critical social theory have been followed, an atmosphere of cooperation will prevail and compromise will be facilitated. All groups will feel they have a stake in the problem-solving process.

Step 8: Quality Control and Continuous Development and Updating

As with any effort, there is a constant need for quality control and continuous development and updating. The process requires meaningful feedback from the relevant groups, the testing of new ideas, and evaluation, as well as individual and group introspection. There is also a need for scientific research, not only on the basic causes of crime and disorder, but also on the effectiveness of the approaches used.

Conclusion

An effective crime and disorder prevention and control effort results only through the cooperative firsthand experience of all relevant groups in the problem-solving process—whether through active involvement or merely through verbalization. This will facilitate cooperation and mutual understanding among the relevant groups.

The most effective means of motivating people is to transmit to them that their opinions will be valued, that they have a voice in decisionmaking, and that they will be involved in the problem-solving process. Efforts will be sponsored and perpetuated if these criteria are adhered to because the parties who comprise the relevant groups have a personal investment in the process. Involved action by the relevant groups will be mutually beneficial and will increase understanding and cooperation among them.

Questions and Answers

What should be done by a police administrator prior to the actual implementation of community policing? There are several steps that are useful. First of all, there should be open community meetings to obtain people's input. Because community policing usually begins on an experimental basis, not all areas of the city or jurisdiction will have a community policing officer. There needs to be justification for placing the officer in a particular beat. The upper command, middle management, and a representation of officers and civilians should be involved in the planning for community policing. Their ideas and input are critical to the success of the effort. After the groundwork is completed, which usually takes from six to eight months, then the actual implementation can take place.

Who should be involved in the planning of community policing? Externally, those persons who are going to be most affected by delivery of the service should be involved in the planning and asked for input. All relevant groups should be involved. Internally, as many rank levels as exist in the department should be represented and involved, and that includes civilian personnel and the union.

How does a community policing officer get input from the community to know what their concerns are? As mentioned above, the most effective way to get input is through face-to-face questioning. However, surveys are more practical, because of the number of people on the beat. Surveys can be done by the officer or they can be conducted by local college students, who can be very effective helpers. This will help develop a profile of what the community sees as important and how they plan to help the officer work to solve problems.

A public forum is a good mechanism to educate the public about community policing. What are the important elements of a forum? There should be a public announcement of the forum, so that there is broad community representation. The media can be used as well as informal methods like word of mouth. Depending on the size the jurisdiction, there may need to be several locations. Usually at least three meetings are necessary. The first session will focus on information dissemination and obtaining general input. The second session, usually at the neighborhood level, will focus on identifying the problems and prioritizing them. The third session will be to develop plans for action with volunteers assigned to dealing with specific concerns. The community policing officer will be the focal point for coordination until residents are comfortable assuming the leadership role.

Why should citizens identify the problems? The citizens are in the best position to know what is needed in their neighborhoods. They also know "what is best" for themselves. If they are asked for their input and are listened to, they will feel needed and have an investment to ensure that problems are solved. They will have a stake in both the process and the outcome.

Why does community policing emphasize getting information from law-abiding citizens? Two groups of people have information that can prevent and solve crime: criminals and law-abiding people. Often it is assumed that only criminals have information about other criminals. Although this is partially true, obtaining information from criminals is often problematic because they may not always be trustworthy. Also, it often means the use of undercover officers to obtain the information, and this can be very dangerous for the officers. Law-abiding people often have the information but are reluctant to reveal it for a variety of reasons. They may not feel their information will make a difference or they may fear retaliation. Once they see that the community policing officer is permanent, trustworthy, and accessible—with a stake in the community—they will transmit information. They begin to feel that the officer is a partner who will help them identify and solve problems.

Is the use of volunteers important to the successful implementation of community policing? Community policing requires the use of volunteers, from volunteers to tutor young people who are headed in the wrong direction to those who are willing to baby-sit for a young mother who is trying to complete high school. A specific example involves responding to a request for assistance in locating a lost Social Security check. The officer can identify the problem, then enlist the support of local church groups and retirees who have experience in working with the bureaucracy to help the elderly person find their Social Security check. If it becomes a criminal matter, then the officer can take further action.

Is there training for community people to help them know how to use their energy to produce positive change in their neighborhoods? There is not much formal training, and some that is available is costly. However, if there is a statewide community coalition, there will be people who are astute and effective at organizing, identifying problems, and coordinating activities for positive action. The federal government also has resources through the Community Relations Division of the Justice Department. Community residents should be "vigilant but not vigilantes." There are also citizen/police academies where citizens learn what the role of the police officer is and what their role as a citizen should be. Find out what training and educational resources exist in your community.

How does community policing prevent vigilantism? Citizens living in problem neighborhoods are often frustrated at the amount of crime and disorder in their area. They lose confidence in the criminal justice system and may feel they need to take the law into their own hands. The community policing officer can give them hope that something will be done, with their help. The community policing officer can tap the energy of the people to direct it into positive channels. Acting as the "pressure cooker release valve," community policing can ensure that the citizens do not do anything illegal and "rash."

Should the police department initiate community policing and then involve the community, or should the community be involved from the start? Ideally, community residents should be involved from the start and, ideally, there should be at least a six-month planning and preparation period before community policing is initiated. Public forums, surveys, and other methods for obtaining citizen input are critical to making the effort a long-term endeavor. It is very important that the community policing officer be in place before "sweep" type operations take place, because the officer will have developed trust with citizens. The community should be given the chance to express concerns and identify important issues and problem people, so that when the sweep takes place they will have a personal stake in seeing that the attempt is successful. The police are usually well aware what must be done, but it is "different" if the citizens tell the police what they need rather than the other way around. It is less patronizing when the citizens identify their own concerns, and they then have more of a stake in the problem-solving process.

How can officers deal with apathetic communities? People are often apathetic unless or until there are high visibility crimes like rapes or robberies going on in their neighborhoods. Unfortunately, once the problem is dealt with effectively, it is often difficult to keep the community "fired up," to continue working on problems so that they do not appear again. That is why it is important to do an initial survey to identify the leaders—the go-getters who are willing to continue in the problem-solving mode even though there might not be a current critical incident. If there are short-, medium- and long-range plans, the chance of continuity increases. Citizens need to understand that just dealing with the symptoms is not the answer. Attainment of long-term goals requires continuous commitment. Communities need to be made safer not just for the present but for the future.

People do not get involved for a variety of reasons, one of them being fear of retaliation from criminals. How do you address this? There is strength in numbers—and when people see that they are not alone in identifying and solving problems, they will become more confident and active. A group leader can be the spokesperson, neutralizing the hostility that may be directed at any one person and projecting to the predators that a group of people are concerned about their deviant behavior. People do not need to "stand alone."

What kind or level of citizen involvement should be expected? There are many different kinds of contributions people can make, ranging from being a leader who organizes block associations, to being the person at home addressing envelopes for a community newsletter, to those who offer firsthand assistance to projects. Not all citizens will be actively involved. Once positive change happens, often more people will get involved.

How can parent/teacher associations get involved with community policing? They should first find out if their area has community policing and then, if it does, find out who the community policing officer is so that they can give input and volunteer to help. If their area does not have community policing, they can call their police department and find out if their area will have community policing in the future.

How does the community policing officer deal with self-proclaimed community leaders? Policing is dependent upon the cooperation of the community. However, in some cases there are persons who call themselves community leaders who may not be. They may even resist the efforts of the officer, especially if the officer is perceived as a community leader and/or begins to operate in a manner that the self-proclaimed leaders do not agree with. Obviously, the officer does not want conflict with any community person, but it may be necessary to deal with these "leaders." A simple community survey can be done, consisting of only four items:

1) What are your concerns?

2) Prioritize those concerns.

3) Which concerns or unmet needs are you willing to work on with the help of the officer?

4) Who are the leaders in the community—the people who get things done, the people who are respected?

Often the persons identified by the survey as leaders are not necessarily those who proclaim themselves to be leaders. Finding out this information can be tactfully used to neutralize the obstructionist self-proclaimed leaders.

Will citizens be patient and wait for their community policing officer if a "regular" officer cannot respond quickly? They will be patient because they know that their community policing officer knows them and their situation. They want to talk with someone familiar with them and their problems. Obviously, however, if it is an emergency they want any officer as soon as possible.

Preparing the Department

For community policing to succeed as a new way of providing police service to the community requires involving everyone in the department. In the three previous sections we discussed the importance of educating all personnel, especially the community policing officer, about how community policing works. In this section, we will discuss how various kinds of training can help everyone in the department acquire the knowledge and skills that they need.

Training in community policing refers primarily to three areas: academy training, field officer training, and ongoing in-service training. Obviously, changes in training must also be part of other internal changes in: recruitment, selection, evaluation, and promotion.*

Free Patrol Time

If community policing is to become a department-wide commitment, it must be expressed by all officers, not just community policing officers. Experience shows that if community policing is viewed internally as a "specialty" assignment, handled by a few, then the rest of the officers will quickly revert to business as usual.

All motor patrol officers should be required to leave their automobiles to interact face-to-face with citizens. This means that officers need "free" (uncommitted) patrol time to be able to leave their cars and work with the community on problem identification and problem solving—and many complain that they do not have enough free patrol time to do so. However, we have found that the real challenge lies in convincing them to use the time that they do have, and this is an example of the kind of problem that can and should be addressed by training.

The solution requires consistency all the way from recruitment through in-service training that will last through the officer's career. If academy trainees have been recruited with the understanding that they will be expected to leave their automobiles on free patrol time,

---

*Note: Ron Sloan of the Aurora, Colorado Police Department contributed to this section. (This first appeared in *The Police Chief,* titled "Basic Issues in Training: A Foundation for Community Policing," August, 1993. Reprinted with permission.)

then they will be more amenable to doing so once out on their own. Academy training can reinforce this expectation by pointing out how face-to-face contact is essential in gaining the trust of citizens, so that the officers can work with people on problem solving.

Then the Field Training Officer (FTO) program should reinforce what was emphasized in academy training. For instance, the FTO should teach by example by exiting the patrol car whenever possible, so that trainees learn to see this as "normal" behavior.

Ongoing in-service training after the academy and the FTO program should not only reinforce the two previous training experiences, but it can be expanded by encouraging officers to share examples about how they solved problems as a result of their involvement with the community. Officers can also talk about how those experiences enhanced their job satisfaction and their perceptions of personal safety, since peer group support is extremely effective, especially among police.

Benefits of Interaction

Officers enjoy their jobs more when they can see that their efforts in working directly with law-abiding people produce concrete, positive results. Decentralized and personalized police service encourages residents to think of officers who patrol their areas as "our" officers—and citizens become protective of their officers. Not only does this make officers feel safer, but residents will indeed come to the aid of an officer in trouble where they might not have before. Exchanging real stories about how community policing enhances problem solving, job satisfaction, and safety is a potent training tool, even more powerful and positive than any kind of formal training through the academy, the FTO program, or in-service training.

If the support and rewards for "out-of-car" interactions are long term and consistent, fewer officers will suffer relapses that will make them want to retreat to the confines of their "office"—the patrol car. With consistent training on this procedure from the start, officers who complain about leaving their cars can be reminded that this was clearly stated as an integral part of the job when they signed on and that this requirement was emphasized all the way through training. In other words, there will be no excuse for officers and their supervisors to grumble about this important aspect of the job.

Parallels to Undercover Work

The interactive approach of community policing parallels that used in undercover work. Therefore, it is ironic that many of the officers who are reluctant to leave their patrol cars are also officers who have worked undercover or wish to do so. Successful undercover officers are rarely in the office. They are out communicating and interacting, using their verbal skills to gather information. When they "make a case," they credit their interpersonal skills with helping them achieve success, and their peer group applauds them for those skills. Over time, as peer group support builds for community involvement, this can legitimize community-based problem solving, just as it legitimizes undercover operations.

The Commitment to Train the Entire Department

Mission-Driven Training

In a community policing department, focusing on the mission of the department rather than its rules requires a dramatic shift in training from a focus on mastery and obedience to a focus on empowerment. This philosophical shift has profound implications for everything that is taught in training, from the academy, through field training, to in-service training. As this suggests, teaching police officers to follow orders and master skills is only useful if used in conjunction with personnel empowerment to fulfill the overarching mission of the department. The officers need to work as partners with people in the community so that they, too, can be empowered to help make their neighborhoods better and safer places.

Any police organization that attempts to institute such a significant philosophical change must establish a comprehensive approach to training that provides the foundation for that change. As expected, many within the department will resist such sweeping change for a variety of reasons, including but not limited to:

- Inherent reluctance to change established attitudes and behaviors.

- Disagreement with the new philosophical approach.

- Misunderstanding of the change implications.

- Perceptions that the change will threaten achieved status.

- Dissatisfaction with training that is not tied directly to mechanical skills, especially those considered as life-saving or those which are tactically based.

All of these obstacles to implementing changes in training must be understood and addressed. However, one of the most troublesome is the latter, because of the particular challenge that it poses to trainers. Police officers, as a whole, are very receptive to hands-on skills training, such as arrest control and defensive tactics, firearms proficiency, high-risk driving techniques, and techniques in the use of intermediate force (batons, chemical agents, etc.). Part of the appeal may well be that the field of policing attracts action-oriented, competitive individuals. Those attributes make it likely that such individuals will enjoy mastering action-oriented skills, where the individual's performance can be measured objectively and his or her final "score" can be clearly assessed and compared to others.

Philosophical, mission-driven training, which forms the conceptual basis for the individual's role as well as the overall organization's collective goals, is often viewed as too theoretical and not useful in any practical sense. The reality, of course, is that most of any officer's daily routine does not include use of deadly force, high-speed pursuits, or physically engaging and restraining unruly citizens. Most of an officer's time is instead spent on taking cold reports, settling civil disputes, motor patrol of assigned areas, or other similar tasks.

If training is to help officers do their best in a community policing department, it should: (1) mirror what it takes to do the actual job well, (2) be informed by the philosophy and mission of community policing, and (3) be structured to maintain the interest of trainees. This is not to say that training should therefore ignore teaching skills such as proficiency in firearms, since such skills can be crucial to the safety and survival of officers and those they are sworn to protect. But traditional training has tended to place less emphasis on skills that might help to defuse potentially dangerous situations before they escalate.

A shift to community policing means balancing reactive efforts with initiatives that emphasize proactive and positive interaction with the community. This means that skills training must reflect the balance of these priorities—for example, by including more focus on improving interpersonal skills. Fulfilling the imperatives listed above means that the entire training area must be informed by the philosophy and mission of the department. A comprehensive approach to training can therefore serve as a foundation for community policing, with the term "comprehensive" used to indicate department-wide training that touches on:

- Introduction or Orientation Training (Sworn and Non-Sworn)
- Basic Academy Training (Sworn)
- Other New-Hire Training (Non-Sworn)
- Police Officer Training (Sworn)
- In-Service Training (Sworn and Non-Sworn)
- Other Specialized Training (Sworn and Non-Sworn)
  —Supervisory
  —Managerial
  —Technical
- Sharing of Current Literature
- Ongoing Information Sharing

A brief description of each area can clarify the basics of a comprehensive training approach.

Introduction or Orientation Training

Implementing the shift to the community policing philosophy must begin with an introduction or orientation to:

- what the philosophy entails,
- how it differs from what is currently being done,
- illustrations of its effectiveness, and
- an overall opportunity for examining the underlying basis for change.

This initial training need not be lengthy, but it should include all department employees, either in the same session or in sessions tailored to each group's specific needs. If we think of a football coach who wants to change his team's approach from a single-wing offense to run-and-shoot, the coach would need to indoctrinate everyone in the organization into accepting the change. Ignoring anyone, from the players to the trainers to the scouts, would jeopardize vital links necessary to produce success for the entire team. Training just the quarterback without training the rest of the players would also ensure disunity—and thereby failure. Likewise, the success of the police department does not rest solely with its officers. The critical functions provided by technical and support personnel require involving them in the process of changing the philosophical approach to line functions.

Basic Academy Training

It is when entry-level police officers join the organization that they are the most open to adopting a philosophical mindset for the police role. Even in situations where recruits have prior experience, they are usually willing to consider subtle changes in their role as they enter a new environment. This is especially true if recruitment, screening, and testing are designed to select individuals with the desire and aptitude for community policing.

The basic academy setting should offer two tracks for community policing training:

"Dedicated" Community Policing Training. This is training specifically devoted to explaining what community policing is and how it works. It would include:

- Brief courses on the philosophy and role of community policing.

- Selected strategies for problem solving and community organization and involvement.

- The philosophy of "accountable creativity" at the line level.

- Other courses, such as mediation and de-escalation of emotionally charged situations (verbal judo, etc.).

Traditional Training. Community policing should be a common thread running through as much of the other training courses as possible. Examples include:

Patrol Procedures—strategies for becoming more community-directed and concerned with quality of life and fear of crime issues while on "normal" patrols. Teaching trainees how to survey residents is useful. Pointing out why responses to citizens such as, "You have been burglarized many times. Why don't you move?" are inappropriate.

Investigations—strategies for engaging residents more effectively in assisting investigations; directing investigative efforts toward identifying the underlying causes of crime and disorder; encouraging trainees to think more broadly.

Traffic Enforcement and Accident Investigation—strategies for diagnosing underlying causes of traffic safety hazards and engaging the community and other service providers in finding resolutions to troubling community traffic safety issues.

Law Enforcement Ethics—establishment of the ethical confines of a law enforcement role in the context of increased community involvement; creative methodologies to increase order maintenance; and the potential for a return to bias, favoritism, and improper use of influence in a community-based model of policing.

Arrest Control and Baton and Defensive Tactics—an underlying philosophical approach to the use of force and physical restraint that includes the principles of the minimum force necessary for humane control; technical proficiency designed to protect officers and citizens alike; and concern for community acceptance of methods.

Department Rules and Directives—an understanding of the framework and rules for the delivery of police service that emphasizes creativity, fairness, community sensitivity, and effective yet humane and acceptable use of force. The reasons underlying the policies and procedures for the organization should always be in concert with the community policing philosophy, and instruction in these areas should emphasize that foundation.

In addition to the above, which necessitate integrating the community policing philosophy into all aspects of department activities, there are some speciality areas that are also important. These skills can be developed and refined prior to entering the academy. Courses can be taken in colleges or through special training programs. However, because all recruits do not have this type of knowledge, the department may have to provide such training. The following are some of the important skills and knowledge areas.

Specialty Areas. Many training programs have instruction in specialty areas already. If not, trainers have other places to turn for assistance. Recruits may be enrolled in relevant courses at a community college, or an instructor of a similar course can be contacted to make presentations.

Consulting firms can also be hired to do the training. Local business executives may be a link to reputable consulting firms. Perhaps a local corporation may already have in-house training personnel who can assist in employee training at reduced or no cost.

Public Speaking. Speaking in public is never easy at first, but anyone with reasonable poise and confidence can learn to do a reasonably good job by following certain rules:

> *Be Prepared.* Thorough preparation is the best antidote to nervousness. Officers should know what they want to get across and to whom. How long do they have to get the message across? Rehearsals help.
>
> *Relax.* Neighborhood gatherings are usually not hostile. People are there because they want to be informed.
>
> *Emphasize Major Points.* Do not spend too much time on minor issues. Emphasize the ideas you want the audience to return home with.
>
> *Do Not Rush.* Speak naturally and pause frequently to illustrate important points with concrete examples.
>
> *Encourage Questions.* Questions provide the opportunity to restate main points and correct false impressions.

Writing Skills. Having good writing skills requires more than just following the conventions of grammar and spelling. The following suggestions may help:

Be Clear. The average reader must be able to understand the presentation. It is, in fact, impossible to be too clear.

Be Natural. Community policing officers are not out to write a Ph.D. dissertation. They write for community residents. The target audience and the issues that concern them should always be kept in mind.

Be Personal. Use the first person singular forms to make your writing more personable (I, you, we).

Seek Help if You Need It. Editors can correct problems with spelling and grammar. Do not be afraid to seek their help if you need it. Many famous authors have been poor spellers.

If you need editorial assistance, ask around in the community. Check some of the following sources for help:

If the work is for a neighborhood publication, that publication may be of assistance.

Some police departments have their own publicists who are equipped with good editorial skills.

Perhaps there is a publicist in another city agency who can help.

Check for editorial volunteers in the neighborhood (free-lance writers, technical writers, journalists).

Perhaps a member of an officer's family or a friend would be willing to help.

Interpersonal Skills/Racial and Ethnic Relations. Written and oral communication skills are more concrete forms of interpersonal skills, but others include imagination, sensitivity, empathy, and sociability. Officers who possess strong interpersonal skills can see where others are "coming from" and know that not all situations can be handled in the same way. Different situations may require different approaches ranging from tact, humor, and diplomacy, to determination and force. Community policing exists to satisfy citizens' unmet needs, but with the lowest level of intervention necessary.

One of the chief interpersonal skills required of a community policing officer is an awareness and sensitivity to racial and ethnic differences, including how they affect the cultural attitudes and differences within a community. Knowing the cultural and historic background of a group can go a long way in explaining its attitudes toward the government in general and the police in particular. Without having this understanding, an officer might have a situation that could lead to undesirable consequences.

- The officer may misinterpret behavior and act harshly when there is no need to.

- The officer may unwittingly antagonize the community.

- The officer who is well meaning but uninformed may be hesitant and uncertain in dealing with an important problem. Not wanting to offend, he or she might not act quickly or decisively.

- The officer may have difficulty mediating a dispute between citizens with different racial or ethnic backgrounds.

Training in the area of interpersonal skills should highlight cultural diversity and expose the dangers of stereotyping and prejudice. The following are some techniques that have effectively imparted racial and ethnic sensitivity in the past:

Case Studies. Trainees should be given a number of real examples of how racial and ethnic sensitivity helped solve a problem, and how a lack of it impeded the solution to a problem or caused further problems.

Role-Playing Scenarios. Dramatization is a powerful training tool. A skillful trainer will have the trainees become involved in the enactment of a scene where racial or ethnic sensitivity is the key to resolving a difficult situation.

Training Films. The trainees can discuss the film and compare their responses with those of the characters on the screen.

Dramatic presentations can enhance readings and lectures, particularly if there is ample time at the end of each presentation to discuss the critical issues that have been raised.

Crisis Intervention. Crisis intervention is central to the duties all police officers, but particularly to the community policing officer. Community policing is proactive—the idea is to intervene before an individual or society is harmed. The high visibility of the community policing officer puts him or her in the unique position to intervene at an early stage of a crisis. Patrol officers lack a certain familiarity with the community and can only act reactively when a crisis becomes serious enough to warrant attention. The hypothetical example below illustrates this and would be helpful in a training session dealing with crisis intervention.

A community policing officer may know a person who has a well-paying factory job. The officer knows also that this person drinks too much and is inclined to become abusive when he does so. Under normal circumstances, this does not prove to be too great a concern. There are occasional embarrassing scenes, but the person manages to stay within the bounds of what is socially tolerable. But suppose, then, that this person loses his job. The behavior may not get worse, but then again it may. The point is that the community policing officer will be aware of the situation and alert for signs of trouble. At the first signs, the officer is in a position to help. The officer may do nothing more dramatic than let the person's spouse know that help is available—leaving the family's dignity intact, while affording them assistance. With intelligence and tact, it is possible to nip the negative behavior in the bud. The following may occur as a result:

— The spouse and family may be spared physical and psychological abuse—perhaps preventing future criminal behavior in the children, as violence at home is often a precursor to criminal behavior as adults.

— The criminal justice system may be spared the cost of taking action against the individual. The community policing officer has intervened in a modest, undramatic way.

— The person may have been spared the trauma of going to jail and is probably more likely to lead a more productive life by having done so.

— The person and/or the family may seek out the officer for future assistance if it is deemed necessary, or they may offer to volunteer in some neighborhood project, if asked.

This example illustrates the ways in which patrol officers are limited—they would only be called to the scene at the point where an incident occurred, such as a domestic violence situation.

Alcohol and drug intervention are the sorts of crises where a community policing officer can make a timely intervention. A community policing officer may also prevent drug experimenters from becoming addicts by helping troubled youngsters find healthy outlets for their energies. An elderly shut-in may get the proper help and attention due to a community policing officer's keen awareness of the community in which he or she walks the beat.

Knowledge of Community Resources and Services. In order to effectively intervene in crises, the community policing officer should know what services—either governmental or private—are available to the community. Services such as legal aid, Alcoholics Anonymous, the Salvation Army, Girl and Boy Scouts, and the American Red Cross may all have local chapters within the community, but the community policing officer should also be familiar with the state and local government programs designed to meet specific needs and to address some of the following problems that commonly arise in troubled neighborhoods:

—lack of food	—financial problems
—lack of shelter	—marital problems
—medical problems	—parenting problems
—legal problems	—transportation problems

Training sessions should include an inventory of the services available to address such problems. If possible, having the directors of the various agencies on hand to answer questions would be ideal.

Developing a community service manual would be a great asset for a community policing officer. Rather than relying on memory, he or she could make referrals to various agencies with full knowledge of the available options and whom to contact about what. Because the services and personnel might change frequently, the manual must be updated periodically. This might be a good first project for the community policing officer to undertake with volunteers from his beat. Having this information on a computer data base with cross referencing would be a great help.

Today's trainees ask more questions, and dialogue about the issues should be encouraged. If academy training emphasizes interaction with trainees, this reinforces the kind of communication and engagement that officers should employ in challenging the community to participate in nominating priorities and fashioning solutions.

Other New-Hire Training

When new non-sworn employees are hired into the organization, special attention should be paid to orienting them toward the mission and role of the department. New support and technical employees need to understand early on that the department is committed to the ideals of community policing. This can help them see how their jobs can support operational efforts to translate the community policing philosophy into practice.

Any new employee who has direct contact with the public (report technicians, dispatchers or complaint clerks, records clerks, receptionists, property and evidence clerks, etc.) should be trained in customer service, and all should be introduced to the concepts of community organization, empowerment and problem solving of community priorities. Many of these employees interact directly with line officers, so it is absolutely imperative that they understand the changing role of the police officer. This understanding will benefit them in providing assistance and support to those line officers.

It cannot be emphasized enough that training civilian police employees is extremely important. They often feel like "second-class citizens." As one civilian dispatcher said, "We had a bomb threat in the building and the building was evacuated except for us. Does that mean that we are expendable?" Dispatchers are important because they not only screen calls and make proper referrals, but they also can explain various options to citizens. For example, they can explain to citizens facing a nonlife-threatening situation that a regular officer can be sent in a relatively short period of time, or, if they are willing to be patient, a community policing officer more familiar with the situation will respond at a later time. Often citizens will be willing to wait because they want an officer familiar with the situation to respond. The dispatcher plays a critical role in the entire process, as do other civilian employees of the department.

Police Officer Field Training

Setting the Tone. The most profound impact on how a police officer works and acts during the early years of his or her career comes from the direction and the example set during field training. Indeed, field training may well be the single most crucial element in changing the culture within the department toward a community policing approach. This "on-the-job" training tends to override whatever trainees learn in academy classrooms, and it sets the stage for what is and is not considered acceptable behavior. Mentoring provided by training officers shapes the strategies, techniques, and, most importantly, the role that recruits embrace. This is particularly true when field training is lengthy, and when it involves daily evaluations and feedback to the trainees.

Because of the tremendous impact that field training has on the entire organization, the philosophical orientation and skills of the training officers are crucial. Therefore, training the trainers in community policing is extremely important if they are to transmit that message to others.

Put bluntly, if an FTO does not both believe in and practice the principles of community policing, it will be virtually impossible for rookies—even those who are enthusiastic about community policing—to perform well following field training that ill prepares them for the job or which undermines their commitment. Since field training is the crucible in which rookies learn what they need to launch their careers, trainers who subvert the principles of community policing, whether consciously or because of lack of proper training themselves, can end up perpetuating the ineffective and outmoded strategies of the professional policing model. For example, trainers can talk all they want to about the virtues of "out-of-automobile" experience, but unless rookies learn by seeing field training officers do this whenever they can, the chances are that rookies will follow the negative example rather than the positive advice.

Job Task Categories. Among the most important changes that must be made in a structured field training program is assessing the job task categories of the daily evaluation to ensure that they reflect the philosophy and practice of community policing. Rectifying problems can require either a redefinition of performance standards under existing job categories (i.e., field performance, investigation, officer safety, interaction with the public, etc.) or even the devising of new job task categories—with corresponding performance standards—that reflect the community policing philosophy, such as:

- *Knowledge and Application of Resources in Daily Work*

    Standards should reflect:
    — An acceptable knowledge base, as reflected in verbal or written tests.
    — Making appropriate referrals on a daily basis.
    — Maintaining a list of appropriate referrals for reference in the field.
    — Taking the time to explain options and resources.
    — Making sure information is correct.

- *Responsiveness to Quality-of-Life Issues in Performance*

    Standards should reflect:
    — General recognition of the importance of quality-of-life issues in the community and the need to address them properly in daily work.
    — Self-initiation of activities such as those listed above.
    — Use of innovative approaches to problem solving.
    — Commitment to the idea of community service, participation, and empowerment.
    — Courtesy, empathy, respect, and helpfulness in daily contacts.
    — Focus on solving problems rather than avoiding them or just taking reports.

- *Relationship with the Community*

    Standards should reflect:
    — Positive interaction with the community.
    — Face-to-face contact with law-abiding citizens whenever possible.
    — Challenging and empowering citizens to participate in nominating and prioritizing problems and in developing short- and long-term solutions.
    — Explaining actions and directions to citizens.
    — Following up on citizen questions and concerns.

It is absolutely essential that management closely supervise the field training program. Weekly evaluations of training officers and sergeants can help ensure that when someone strays off track from the community policing model, he or she can be redirected quickly. Additionally, field training sergeants must lead both the trainers and recruits by example during the daily activities encountered on the street.

In-Service Training

Maintaining and Reinforcing Momentum. Achieving change is difficult, but maintaining change and empowering employees to pursue new techniques or skills is impossible without a mechanism for continual reinforcement. Formal in-service training provides a way to maintain momentum and to build new skills. Unfortunately, many organizations provide little refresher training, or such training is directed only at sworn officers. Not only should training be provided to both sworn and non-sworn personnel, but it should be infused with and devote sessions to the principles and strategies of community policing.

Workshops on community organization, empowerment, problem solving, special projects, performance evaluation guidelines, and local and national updates on police strategies can be structured to suit the needs of both sworn and non-sworn personnel, depending on the needs and constraints of the organization. Of overriding importance is that police managers understand that in-service updates are critical to institutionalizing community policing.

Other Specialized Training

Educating Supervisors and Managers. Overlooking the need to provide specialty training risks dooming attempts to institutionalize community policing. Not only must first-line supervisors be able to recognize and reward community empowerment and creative problem solving, but they must be trained to encourage risk-taking and innovation among subordinates. At issue as well is the fact that risk-taking and innovation depend on mutual trust between supervisors and line officers. Without such trust, line officers will stick with the status quo, which typically rewards those who do not make any waves (which means they take no chances).

Supervisors and managers must be willing to accept honest mistakes, or line officers will continue to rely on conventional strategies that ultimately lead to stagnation. Accountable risk-taking emphasizes responsibility, not license, and it examines failures or mistakes as a means of learning how to do better in the future, not as a means of assigning blame. Managers in a community policing department can specifically benefit from skills training in redirecting, leading by example, and constructive criticism (coaching and facilitation).

Managers and command officers should also be given the opportunity to understand and facilitate the philosophical change to community policing. Without repeated training, top leaders in the department can see community policing as a threat to their status and power. Again, training must emphasize that community policing means that all functions in the department are driven by the mission, not by the rules, and this means that the role of police managers must change from that of "controller" to "facilitator." Unless this problem is addressed, top-level support can wane—undermining and even sabotaging the entire effort.

Other areas of specialized skills training include:

- Application of performance assessment systems.
- Development of community policing goals and objectives.
- How to organize and facilitate community self-help groups.
- Public speaking.

Sharing of Current Literature and Documentation. The explosion in new information on community policing can make it difficult to stay abreast of what is happening in the field. Therefore, departments should consider establishing a system to gather materials, to assess their usefulness, and then to make them widely available. A central repository or library of articles, research, video and audio tapes, and books can serve as a valuable training resource for the entire department. The department should also maintain contact with the National Center for Community Policing, the Police Executive Research Forum, the Police Foundation, the International Association of Chiefs of Police, the National Institute of Justice, and other national organizations to ensure receiving new publications as they become available.

Ongoing Information Sharing. As efforts to shift to community policing gain momentum, the department should explore methodologies for sharing information on strategies and projects with others inside and outside the department. This is important for many reasons. First, disseminating this information can make it possible for others to borrow useful ideas. Second, it can help reinforce the message that community policing works. Third, it provides recognition for individuals and groups who deserve praise for their initiative. Fourth, documenting success to groups outside the department can help to build broad-based support— among political leaders, business owners, community leaders, taxpayers and voters, other government agencies, non-profit groups, and average citizens.

Many departments have produced newsletters and videos, and some have established computerized databases. A database accessible throughout the department can make it easier to avoid the need to "reinvent the wheel" each time someone is looking for possible solutions to community problems, but departments that cannot afford that luxury must find some way to gather and disseminate this kind of useful information.

Conclusion to Training

The Function of Training. Training is crucial for the adoption of any significant change, and it is the foundation for how we respond to challenges, both individually and collectively. A comprehensive training approach is essential in institutionalizing the philosophy and practice of community policing within a police agency.

Community Input. Also important is the need to solicit the community's input into the training of line officers, since their help can be invaluable in designing training that meets their needs and expectations.

Training and Selection. The new role expectations for community policing officers have obvious implications for selection and training. For instance, considering the superior communication skills that community policing officers need raises the issue of whether such skills should be a precondition of employment or whether training should be targeted to remedy any deficiencies after hiring.

If the decision is that these skills should be dealt with in training after the candidate is hired, that raises a new set of issues that must be resolved: If communication skills training is added to basic training, what other subjects should be dropped or reduced to make room? Should such classes be offered in addition to the existing program? If so, what are the cost implications?

Perhaps such training should be offered as part of advanced training. Again, this leads to other questions: Should classes be conducted in formal classroom sessions? Or should they be part of roll call, with trainers brought in or with lessons on video or computer? Another option might be to offer self-paced home-study materials. And again, what are the cost implications?

Other Subject Areas. As this shows, dealing with even one skill area raises questions about others—and community policing officers need many new skills. A case can be made that community policing officers would benefit from additional training in:

foreign languages	child psychology and development
basic psychology	political science
human relations	urban planning
gerontology and the problems of aging	city management

It requires little imagination to come up with an intriguing roster of classes, yet the question remains regarding how much training. Unless you can afford to expand training, adding something new to the roster implies short shrift for something else. Obviously, the training roster cannot be determined simply by allocating training time according to how officers spend most of their time. For example, officers spend less than 1% of their time administering first-aid or firing a weapon, yet those are skills that they must learn to perform well or people can die.

The challenge requires balancing traditional and non-traditional training and ensuring that the community policing philosophy infuses both. If all the worthwhile skills cannot be added to basic training, there may be ways to provide them in advanced training or through self-paced studies, by assigning trainers to roll call, or by providing training through new technologies like video and audio cassettes and computers.

Conclusion

Revising training so that the entire department understands community policing and receives help in building the knowledge and skills required is an ambitious goal. Again, this is part of why departments report that making the transition takes years to accomplish. The purpose in exploring training from various perspectives is to identify ways in which community policing can inform the entire training curriculum over time.

Questions and Answers

What percentage of the department should be committed to community policing?
Community policing in the long run is supposed to be a total departmental commitment. It should involve everyone in the department including investigators, civilians, and all employees. In practice, departments cannot totally change overnight to community policing; thus it is necessary to begin on an experimental basis. Most communities start out, again depending on size, with one or two

experimental beat areas. After its effectiveness is demonstrated to the public, the media, and the other officers, that can then be expanded to more beats, and ultimately the entire city will be covered—with everyone acclimated to community policing. In Lansing, the community policing officers attempt to integrate the regular three-shift permanent officers into the community policing process, so that ultimately the community policing officers put themselves out of business and the regular officers handle all community policing.

How do investigators fit into the community policing philosophy? Community policing should be a department-wide philosophy and involves more than just community policing officers and/or patrol officers; it should involve every division, ranging from traffic officers to investigators. Investigators, for example, should be kept informed and in the loop relative to what community policing officers are doing and the important information they develop. In addition, investigators periodically can be put in uniform to patrol the areas and remember what it is like to be on patrol. This keeps them acclimated to the community policing concept in a very direct fashion. Some departments have decentralized investigators so that they work side by side with the community policing officer.

Is having a job description/role definition of great importance prior to initiating community policing? It is very important that the officer have a job description and role definition that is different from traditional patrol prior to going into the beat. This provides a reference point for the officer so that he or she knows what is expected and thus can be evaluated according to that reference point. It is important for the community to know what the officer's role and function is so that they do not misuse the officers by, for example, wanting them to provide security for only certain areas of the neighborhoods. It provides the officer the hedge against school people wanting the officer to be their disciplinarian or from business people wanting the officer to patrol primarily around their business.

How much experience should an officer have before being placed in community policing? This varies widely because some of the best officers have been those who have several years of experience, and who may have even been cynics originally. These experienced officers have often turned out to be the most committed, dynamic officers in the community. On the other hand, very young officers also turn out to be very effective. The general rule is that an officer should have some experience, generally two to three years, so that he or she is comfortable with general departmental policies and procedures, basically knows the streets of the community, and knows the rudimentary elements of police work and is comfortable with the job. In addition, the officer needs to have enough experience to know what police work really involves, and that it is not just chasing crooks. Regardless of the experience of the officer, he or she needs to be someone who: is comfortable working both one-on-one and in groups, likes to ask questions and get input and is not autocratic, is willing to see what the resources of the community are, knows what the community agencies are and what their role should be, is comfortable talking to the media—in general, someone who likes people.

Is the community policing officer a generalist or a specialist? Community policing requires officers who are skilled in several areas. They are generalists and can function in a broad fashion, often limited only by the union contract. They diagnose the strengths and weaknesses of the neighborhoods, enlist the support and input of citizens, and jointly develop a plan of action. They try to prevent crime, but once it occurs they respond with the necessary action. Overall, however, community policing officers are full-service police officers.

How far should this generalist orientation go with community policing? The community policing officer is expected to do as much as possible to identify and solve crime and disorder problems. Obviously the officer cannot "be all things to all people" and be knowledgeable in all aspects of crime prevention, detection, and resolution. The officer, for example, will usually not be astute at investigating homicides, arsons, and other "speciality" crimes.

Should community policing officers be matched with beats on the basis of race? The question is often asked if the officer should be of the same race as the majority of the people that he or she will serve. When a black officer is put in a predominantly black area or a white officer in a predominantly white area, this may enhance the initial rapport between the officer and the community, but in the long run it makes no difference because citizens want quality service regardless of the race of the officer. So an officer should not be selected primarily because of race. However, if a community speaks a particular language like Spanish, it is useful to have an officer, regardless of race, who can speak that language. Increasingly there are southeast Asian communities that have difficulty relating to police for a variety of reasons. Someone who can speak the language, or at least understand part it, is very useful. Officers who understand the people, their culture, and their needs are most effective.

Should community policing officers be members of special tactic teams like S.W.A.T.? Being on a S.W.A.T. team is not antithetical to community policing. Community policing requires officers that are committed to full-service policing. Most departments do not have full-time S.W.A.T. teams, so part-timers are used. S.W.A.T. training includes many of the elements and characteristics desired in community policing. For example, an effective S.W.A.T. team member is able to evaluate a situation and make a decision based on a wide range of alternatives, such as whether to enter a dwelling or whether to wait for several hours, even days. The S.W.A.T. person needs to be able to communicate over a telephone, loudspeaker, or even face to face. The S.W.A.T. person needs good information from neighbors and their trust, possibly even using one their houses as a command post. These are some of the characteristics necessary for effective community policing.

What is the ideal training for a community policing officer? There is no "ideal" training, because community policing needs to reflect the strengths and weaknesses of the particular neighborhood(s). However, the officer should understand the basic principles and elements, and know that it is a philosophy and not just an isolated program. Although classroom training is useful, on-the-job training is probably the best. If a department already has community policing on an experimental basis, new community policing officers can be trained by the veteran community policing officers. If the department does not have community policing, then they can send their new officers to another community to learn community policing from an experienced community police officer. The beauty of this approach is that the officers can exchange ideas and learn from each other.

What are some of the skills that a community policing officer should have? Obviously, he or she should like people and desire to be the best public servant possible. Fine-tuned police skills are a must. In addition, it is helpful if the officer is comfortable using modern technology like a computer, has good interpersonal skills, is an effective report writer, and knows a foreign language or is willing to learn the rudiments of one if he or she works in a neighborhood where many people speak a different language.

Does emphasizing a "new breed" of officer mean that past and present officers are not suited for community policing? Every police department, especially the smaller ones, usually has some people doing some form of community policing. It has just never been institutionalized as a departmental philosophy. The majority of officers currently serving can effectively do community policing. They need to be rewarded for doing it and given the flexibility to be a professional, which means being trusted. Those officers who are not acclimated to the approach can be given other assignments. New persons "coming in the front door" can be screened for their receptivity to community policing with the knowledge that the organization has the philosophy as the core of its operation.

Do you need officer visibility with community policing? It is a different kind of community visibility, not the traditional officer in the car in uniform. The community police officer will, for example, be visible at community meetings and doing personal and business security checks, being at schools, and attending other functions. It is the actions of community policing officers that makes them visible, not their mere presence in uniform.

Should the department treat community policing officers differently? Community policing officers get rewards in several ways, ranging from flexible schedules to receiving awards. In addition, the citizens make them feel good by giving them compliments and support. One department gave its community policing officers a special raise. However, that may be counterproductive because it may foster antagonism with the rest of the officers in the department.

What will some of the concerns be when implementing community policing? One major concern is the safety of the officers. Without overstating what happens, once the officer is integrated into the community, he or she becomes "our officer." The community then becomes the greatest protector of the officer by, for example, informing the community policing officer that there are persons in the community who are a threat to the officer. Our research has demonstrated over the years that the safety of the officers is increased because the people look out for them. Another concern is whether the officer will do "real" police work. Community policing officers should make arrests when needed and not just depend on regular officers. They should function as full-service officers.

If an officer is too successful in a high-crime rate area, can there be a danger to the officer? Effective officers often get threats and even death threats. In one community, an officer received a death threat from drug dealers. The police department saturated the area with many more officers to project that they were not going to be intimidated. The citizens also responded by walking the beat with the officer and producing information that led to the arrest of the perpetrators.

Is street survival training for community policing officers inconsistent with community policing? Community policing officers need to know who the "good guys" and the "bad guys" are in the neighborhoods. They do not need to be defensive and suspicious with the law-abiding people. With the nonlaw-abiding, they need all of the help they can get, ranging from citizen help to a knowledge of techniques that will help them survive on the street.

How do you deal with prejudiced officers? No doubt, many departments have hired individuals who have hidden prejudices towards one group or another, but the issue is not what the person thinks or feels but what he or she does on the job. If people allow their personal feelings to influence their behavior, their misbehavior must be uncovered and dealt with. If they can overcome their biases and behave appropriately on the job, difficult as that may be, then sometimes their personal feelings and attitudes are irrelevant. Many times when a prejudiced officer's behavior changes, he or she will be better received by citizens—and this may have the effect of changing the officer's negative attitudes.

Will community policing officers make mistakes if they are given the freedom and flexibility to be innovative and creative? Whenever someone is given the opportunity to do things differently and take risks there is the chance that mistakes will be made. Supervisors need to treat the officer like a professional and, the vast majority of the time, the officer will behave appropriately and even creatively. If a well-meaning mistake is made, the officer should be supported and helped to learn from the mistake.

Do community policing officers get better information than their counterparts in other units? The essence of community policing is partnership, and a true partnership only happens when people trust each other. If community policing is working the way it should, then there should be a partnership and trust with the ultimate result being that there is an exchange of information, sometimes even better information than that received by officers in other units.

Does job satisfaction improve for community policing officers? Because the community policing officer has a stake in the neighborhood, he or she becomes trusted and respected. He or she is "our officer." The officer gets much support and is often viewed as a hero because of the leadership shown in solving crime and disorder problems. Compliments are often "few and far between" with traditional policing because citizens do not have a long-term relationship with those officers. With community policing, the officer is known and respected, resulting in positive feedback and compliments.

Do the good efforts of a community policing officer sometimes not get generalized to other members of the department? In one community, the Spanish-speaking citizens liked and trusted their officer so much (even though he was not Spanish speaking) that they would not call the "regular" police and always depended on "their" officer. One day an elderly resident had a heart attack and the citizens would not call an emergency vehicle or a "regular" officer. They looked for their community policing officer and, by the time he arrived, the man had died. That is a case of placing too much trust in the officer at the expense of not generalizing that trust to all public safety providers. In the interim before community policing is department-wide, it is hoped that the positive efforts of community policing officers will be generalized to the other industrious and dedicated officers in the community.

What Community Policing Officers Do on the Job

In too many cases, officers are told, "You are now a community policing officer—go do the job," as if that is all the guidance and direction that they need to succeed. The reality, of course, is that community policing officers will continue to need assistance even beyond the training discussed in Section Four.

Because community policing is a philosophy, not a program, many of the intangibles involved in the job cannot be captured on paper. Community policing officers need to be receptive to input and ideas from citizens, and they must be creative and innovative in translating that input into actions that help to solve the problems that the community faces. Community policing officers also need freedom and autonomy—including the freedom to fail.

The job also requires flexibility in scheduling. Community policing officers often organize community events that bring the neighborhood together, and coordinating such events typically requires working during regular business hours. Yet the officer may need the freedom and flexibility to work in the evenings, such as when there is a crack house to be raided. This requires a great deal of trust between community policing officers and their supervisors. Trust is essential, since the officer must have the freedom to do what is best for the neighborhood, although it may not fit exactly into traditional scheduling patterns.

Thus community policing is a mindset and not just an officer doing on foot what is normally done in an automobile. For example, consider the following description used by the Michigan State University Police:

> Community policing is the philosophy of involving a police officer in a specific section of the community, with ownership, on a long-range basis. The key element is geographic ownership. The community policing officer works to organize the resources of the community, the police department and other agencies to reduce crime and meet the appropriate needs of the community.

> Community policing is a philosophy of caring, working with people and helping people. This often means helping people informally when the formal systems do not seem to work.

In the above example, note the emphasis on community policing as a philosophy, not just a program, and the emphasis on the community policing officer as an organizer of other resources, not someone who performs individual tasks. This mindset forms the basis of how the community policing officer approaches actually performing his or her job.

This section will look first at the basic duties and activities of community policing officers. It will show how these elements can be fashioned into a specific job description, which departments can tailor to their requirements. A closer look is given at how community policing officers directly apply the concept of community-based problem solving in their daily work, including a discussion of logistics—about the beat itself, establishing an office, introducing the officer to the community, the Neighborhood Network Center concept, and so on. With that fuller understanding of what the job of community policing officer entails, you will clearly see the implications for the selection process.

General Duties and Activities

Several years have been spent collecting information on what community policing officers do. The following list represents the general categories of duties and activities:

Law Enforcement. The community policing officer performs general duties common to all police patrol assignments.

Directed Patrol. Though increased visibility on the street is an added plus, the main reason for removing the community policing officer from the patrol car is to allow the officer the time and opportunity to work behind the scenes, involving the community in efforts to make the beat a better and safer place in which to live and work.

Community Involvement. The community policing officer attempts to build an atmosphere of mutual respect and trust, so that average citizens and community leaders form a new partnership with the police, to address the problems of crime, drugs, fear of crime, and social and physical disorder, including neighborhood decay.

Identifying and Prioritizing Problems. The community policing officer works with community residents to identify and prioritize problems.

Reporting. The community policing officer shares information, including information about problems in the beat, with officers who are part of the team and also with the rest of the department, including special units (such as narcotics).

Problem Solving. Because of the knowledge that the community policing officer has of the neighborhood and the people who live there, he or she can be the catalyst to develop creative solutions to problems that do not focus exclusively on arrest.

Organizing. The community policing officer rapidly moves beyond organizing activities such as Neighborhood Watch to organizing a number of community-based initiatives and activities aimed at specific problems and at enhancing the overall quality of life in the community.

Communicating. The community policing officer gives formal and informal talks to individuals and groups to educate people about crime prevention techniques and to discuss problems in the beat. He or she also employs writing skills to communicate with residents in the beat and may also be empowered to communicate directly with the media.

Conflict Resolution. The community policing officer mediates, negotiates, and resolves conflicts formally and informally (and challenges people to begin resolving problems on their own).

Referrals. The community policing officer refers problems to appropriate agencies: code enforcement, social services, drug treatment, animal control, sanitation, and so on.

Visiting. The community policing officer makes home and business visits to acquaint individuals in the beat with community policing, to enlist their help, and to educate them about crime prevention.

Recruiting and Supervising Volunteers. The community policing officer must solicit, train, and supervise paid and/or unpaid community volunteers, ranging from individuals who assist with clerical duties to people who are working with juveniles in the neighborhood.

Proactive Projects. In addition to efforts that focus on solving immediate problems, the community policing officer works with the community on short-term and long-term efforts to prevent problems and enhance the quality of life.

Targeting Special Groups. Part of the community policing officer's mandate is to protect and assist groups with special needs—women, juveniles, the elderly, the disabled, and the homeless, as well as to target other groups such as youth gangs for special attention.

Targeting Disorder. Unlike traditional police officers, the community policing officer's mandate includes emphasis on developing solutions to problems of social and physical disorder and neighborhood decay.

Networking with the Private Sector. The community policing officer contacts and solicits the active participation of business, ranging from donations of goods from small business to broad corporate support for new initiatives.

Networking with Non-Profit Agencies. The community policing officer acts as both liaison and facilitator with non-profit agencies, ranging from food banks to the Boy Scouts and Girl Scouts.

Administrative/Professional Duties. The community policing officer participates in training, roll call, and office duties (answering mail, phone call, reports).

The information above describes general duties and activities, but community policing officers need more specific reference points so that they can tell whether they are performing to the expectations of both the department and the community. A job description not only offers the officer much-needed guidance, but it also provides supervisors the basis for assessing the officer's performance.

Without a clear job description, community policing officers can stray across dangerous lines without realizing that they are doing so. In one department where there was no job description for community policing officers, an officer became actively involved in a partisan voter registration campaign initiated by an ambitious candidate seeking to dislodge the incumbent. Needless to say, the incumbent, his political party, city hall, and police officials were furious—and the entire community policing effort was halted.

It is very important that prior to assigning a community policing officer to a beat that he or she be given a job description. The job description should not be so specific that it stifles creativity, but it should be specific enough so that it provides guidance. The following is an example of a workable job description.

Sample Specific Job Description

The community policing officer will be responsible for a variety of duties that will include, but not be limited to, the following:

- Perform the duties of a police officer assigned to the Uniform Patrol Bureau as necessary.

- Gather and report intelligence-related information in reference to the officer's assigned neighborhood.

- Provide a sense of security for businesses and citizens within the assigned neighborhood.

- Become acquainted with the merchants, businesses, and citizens within the neighborhood and assist them in identifying problem areas or concerns.

- Enforce local and state laws, particularly those related to, or specifically drafted for, the assigned neighborhood.

- Respond when available to all calls for service within the assigned neighborhood.

- Respond when available and investigate reports of criminal offenses within the assigned neighborhood.

- Be responsible for building security, where applicable—particularly vacant or temporarily closed businesses and residences.

- Develop and conduct speaking presentations on topics that have been identified as concerns and/or problems within the neighborhood.

- Research and develop materials for preparing outlines, newsletters, and citizen training programs, as well as in-service training programs.

- Conduct interviews with representatives of the media.

- Serve as a member of various organizations and committees at the direction of the administration.

- Conduct security surveys, complete crime risk reports, and provide follow-up contacts on commercial/residential burglaries and armed robberies that occur within the assigned neighborhood.

- Prepare and coordinate the tasks to be accomplished within the neighborhood on a weekly basis.

- Prepare weekly evaluation reports describing task accomplishments related to program goals and objectives.

- Coordinate the services of various governmental and private agencies in an effort to resolve identified problems within the neighborhood.

- Organize resources of the community, the police department and other agencies to reduce crime and meet the appropriate needs of the community.

- Due to the nature of the assignment, it is anticipated that the officer selected will have to work a flexible schedule of 40 hours per week with variable leave days. Authorized functions or activities above 40 hours will be compensated as overtime.

Community-Based Problem Solving

The list of general duties and activities and the specific job description together provide a basic picture of what community policing officers do and what is expected of them. However, most community policing officer candidates still want examples of community-based problem solving.

Examples of Community-Based Problem Solving

Since creativity is an essential ingredient in community-based policing, and because all initiatives must take into account the needs of the community, there is simply no way to provide an exhaustive list of examples. Offered instead are some ideas, grouped by various kinds of common problems and concerns. Keep in mind that some of these examples can also be applied to other circumstances. The purpose of this listing is not to limit your imagination but to prime it.

Problem Identification. These initiatives can help community policing officers introduce themselves to the community, so that they can begin to build the rapport necessary for the community to share their concerns.

- Door-to-door drop-off of business card/flyer with telephone number of community-based office.

- Use of community surveys to learn about unreported crime and other problems.

- Attendance at local meetings, church activities, and social events.

- Use of transportation that makes community policing officers aware of the environment and easily approachable, such as bicycles, all-terrain vehicles, horses, and golf carts.

- Involvement in established activities such as Special Olympics.

- Use of the media to provide safety tips, especially at special times of the year such as Halloween.

Disorder. Community policing officers can employ various approaches to identify and deal with disorder.

- Surveillance (with or without a camera) at peak times of disorder.

- Promote enactment of loitering laws; post "No Parking or Standing" signs; enforce park restrictions on hours and alcohol.

- Community cleanup of vacant lots that attract drug dealers and prostitutes.

- Work with code enforcement to tear down abandoned buildings that can become havens for problem people.

- Work with churches, businesses, and volunteers to provide secure shelter for the homeless, to gather donated clothes, to help at soup kitchens.

- Identify absentee landlords and hold them accountable for code violations and unkempt lots.

- Tow abandoned vehicles used by prostitutes.

- Supervise offenders on probation and parole and those sentenced to community service.

Anti-Drug Initiatives. Community policing officers can be a catalyst in addressing street-level drug problems.

- Organize and supervise citizen groups to patrol streets where drug dealers operate.

- Work with landlords and attend apartment showings to discourage dealers from moving in.

- Establish drug hotlines for anonymous tips.

- Use forfeiture laws against landlords who cater to drug dealers.

- Remove pay telephones (or limit them to outgoing calls) to discourage use by drug dealers.

- Connect addicts, particularly priority addicts such as pregnant women, with drug treatment facilities (cutting red tape where possible).

- Post lists of jobs available in the community-based office and warn known dealers to find other work or face arrest.

- Institute D.A.R.E. officers in schools.

- Provide positive alternative activities/groups for youngsters at risk of joining gangs.
- Work with apartment managers/private security to establish a resident I.D. system to keep drug dealers/customers out of problem facilities.

At-Risk Youths.

- Organize activities/classes designed to instill self-esteem.
- Work with recreation personnel and volunteers to expand after-school and summer sport activities.
- Recruit volunteers for tutoring and post a list in the community-based office.
- Encourage schools to stay open late—and recruit volunteers—so that youngsters have a place to socialize other than the street.
- Educate youths on their legal rights and responsibilities.
- Initiate conversations about child abuse to uncover hidden problems. Be alert for signs of abuse. Organize classes for parents on dealing with stress.
- Encourage schools/churches to provide "quiet rooms" where youngsters can do their homework.
- Involve parents in enforcing curfews.
- Work with area businesses/residents on providing safe havens for children.
- Encourage churches to develop an exchange program so that urban youth can visit rural/suburban areas and vice versa.
- Enlist university arts/literature departments to establish classes so that youngsters can express themselves.

Women.

- Conduct rape prevention classes.
- Establish a volunteer escort service to accompany women at night.
- Make a concerted outreach to inform women about services and facilities.

The Elderly.

- Provide information on "cons" aimed at the elderly.
- Recruit volunteers to accompany and assist them on shopping trips.
- Enlist older citizens as volunteers to work with at-risk youths.

In addition to the community policing officer's direct involvement with the above groups, he or she can also enlist the assistance of others in the community. For example, one community policing officer identified all of the elderly in her area that were housebound because of physical problems or because of fear of crime. She asked the local mail carrier to do a quick check on them when the mail was delivered through a system of either waving through the window or making quick face-to-face contact to make sure that they were okay. The firefighters at the neighborhood firestation were also willing to make daily telephone calls to the approximately 20 persons identified in order to ensure that they were okay. (Some of these firefighters were also willing to talk to latchkey kids after school.) In addition, the officer contacted the local high school social sciences teacher, and as a community project his students would do grocery shopping for the infirmed and volunteer for other activities such as raking leaves and shoveling snow.

There is a tremendous amount of volunteer help that can assist the officer in dealing with the problems of the community. The officer cannot possibly do all of the cleanups and the telephone calling, make daily contact with the elderly, and directly work on other community projects without help. However, the community policing officer can identify and organize the residents.

Logistical Issues

Identifying Beats: Community of Interest

The last section listed the criteria for prioritizing areas that request or need community policing. The community policing officer is usually not the one to develop these classifications, although he or she may have been input in the planning process. Having a priority list is important because community policing will take years to be instituted throughout an entire department. Therefore most departments begin on an experimental basis, often one beat at a time. If the method for selecting the beats is not perceived as fair, there will be competition throughout the city and accusations of political favoritism. Obviously the officer assigned to a particular beat should not be caught in the middle of the politics involved.

Determining Beat Boundaries

As Section Three pointed out, the ideal in determining beats is to have distinct geographic boundaries that identify neighborhoods occupied by persons with similar characteristics. The ideal is not usually achievable, however, because the area is rarely defined by distinct boundaries such as rivers and railroad tracks and because most communities are diverse. Therefore beat boundaries are usually determined according to a "community of interest," particularly based on concerns about crime and disorder. Often a public housing tract is considered the beat boundary; in other cases, it is an area surrounding a school, church, or an ethnic or racial enclave that exhibits some cohesiveness. There may be areas that are "natural neighborhoods" by history, development, geography, or ethnicity. Once the boundaries have been determined, some officers hold a "name your neighborhood" contest to increase the sense of pride and ownership within the community.

Optimal Size of the Beat

When the beat area is too large, the community policing officer is overwhelmed and cannot maintain the daily face-to-face contact so important in community policing. It is difficult to generalize about the optimal size for every beat, because size is dependent upon population density, geographic size, amount of crime and disorder, number of perpetrators frequenting the area, number of high-rise buildings, number of businesses, number of young people, number of transients, cohesiveness of the community, as well as many other factors.

One rule of thumb is to have the beat area small enough so that the officer can walk every street (or every floor of a high rise building) once every three days. Another guideline is that the officer should be able to knock on every door in the area within an eight-month period (recognizing that not everyone will be home at the time of the attempted contact.)

If the area is densely populated, the beat might include only a block or two. If the area consists of single homes on large lots, the beat may be many blocks. A larger geographic area may require that the officer use a bike, a motor scooter, or some other vehicle to patrol the area. In these larger geographic areas, using a car but parking and walking is obviously the most efficient method, as long as the officer is not continually tied to the radio.

"Park and walk," although very efficient, has its problems because the officer needs to have the mindset that being out of the automobile is as important as being in it. Many officers are reluctant to leave their patrol cars—not only because they feel it is inefficient but because they may get a call or because they fear for their safety, even though it is becoming increasingly clear that officers who are deeply involved in a regular beat area are safer because citizens will come to their aid in time of crisis.

It is better to have an area that turns out to be too small than an area so large that an officer cannot get the community stabilized. In one community, the beat area started with 500 households, because it was a high-crime area. After the area was stabilized, the beat size was doubled the following year.

In the exuberance to begin community policing with limited resources, a common mistake is to make the area too large. This makes it very difficult for the officer and citizens to identify and deal with problems on a long-term basis.

Selecting an Office: Decentralization

One of the important elements of community policing, especially in larger jurisdictions, is decentralization. It is important that the officer be accessible and accountable to the citizens. This usually necessitates the officer having an office in the neighborhood, although this is not as important in smaller jurisdictions where the officer is accessible at the central location. (However, even in these cases, some people are reluctant to go to a central location). A decentralized office encourages dialogue, even though most of the community policing officer's time will be spent out of the office.

The location of the office in the neighborhood is not as important as the need for it to be accessible. The office can be in a(n):

- School
- Recreation center

- Donated apartment within private or public housing

- Church office

- Forfeited and remodeled drug house

- Mobile home trailer

Having an office in a trailer, however, might send the message that the community policing effort is not permanent and can be interrupted at any time. Permanency is important, so that community policing is not perceived as just another short-term government experiment.

Many community policing officers have been successful at securing donated space and supplies from concerned business people, churches, schools, or other organizations. In fact, one way to bring the neighborhood together is to organize a fund-raiser such as a rummage sale or bake sale for the money to equip the office and even to pay for telephone and utility bills. In one city, civic agencies such as Kiwanis and Rotary adopted specific community police offices and paid telephone and office expenses. In another instance, a school designated all proceeds from a school soft drink vending machine to be used to support the local community policing officer's phone expenses. Neighborhood residents may even volunteer their time and skills to decorate, clean, and maintain the office space.

Other than the basic office furniture, a telephone, and answering machine for when the officer and volunteers are out of the office, the officer might benefit from some or all of the following:

office supplies	business cards
photocopier	information handouts
fax machine	bicycle, scooter or horse

What the Officer Should Do First

Once the beat has been identified and an office selected, the newly assigned community policing officer should take at least two weeks to become familiar with the area and its people. Recommended "get started" activities include the following.

- Take one to two days to ride around the area alone, getting to know the geography and the landmarks. Study a map. Note the locations of churches, businesses, agencies and schools.

- Develop your own personal "letter of introduction." The letter should introduce you by name, and it should stress friendliness, informality, and a first-name-basis relationship. It should outline your duties as a community policing officer and provide your local office phone or pager number. Emphasize that, in an emergency, people should dial 911, so the closest police will respond. For long-range crime and neighborhood problems, people can contact you directly as their own neighborhood community policing officer. (See Appendix C for a sample letter of introduction.)

- After a couple of days, make contact with area clergy, business owners, local agencies, and school officials.

- Walk the entire area and begin to meet people at random, explaining that you are a full-service community policing officer who has been assigned to the area on a long-term basis and that you have an office in the neighborhood (giving them the location), hand out your business card, mention that you will be responding to calls when you are on duty, and explain about your answering machine. It is important to mention that you are working closely with the regular motorized officers and that they will be integrated into this approach.

- Discuss how formal survey material will be distributed, so that all residents will have a chance to identify problems, prioritize them, and discuss which ones they are willing to help with. (See Appendix D for a sample survey.)

- Make motor patrol officers in your area aware of your presence and keep them informed about what you are doing. Information can be shared formally (memos, messages, role call) or informally (in conversations over coffee or lunch).

- Community policing officers should be supplied with a crime analysis report for the area and an estimate of unreported crime as a baseline to compare how much the reporting of crime increases over time, as an indicator of whether trust is building.

Introduction to the Community

After taking a week or two to familiarize himself or herself with the general area, the officer should begin going door to door, introducing himself or herself to whomever answers and explaining his or her role. If no one is home, a business card or letter of introduction should be left in the door.

Consideration should be given to other creative ways of introduction. Perhaps enlisting a Scout troop to hand out flyers, or posting them at convenience stores and laundromats. Officer Don Reynolds took a novel approach by writing and recording a rap song that he called "Reynolds Rap," which he played on a boom box as he walked the beat. Area kids followed him, laughing and pointing. Soon, however, they could not resist asking him what he was doing, and experience shows that if you make friends with youngsters, their parents will follow.

Daily Routine Activities

Even though the job of being a community policing officer requires flexibility, the officer will typically establish some sort of routine. While the routine may vary somewhat from day to day, a daily routine can help officers organize their time. Many community policing officers begin the shift by listening to messages on the answering machine, making callbacks, attending to business left over from the previous day, and handling paperwork. With the office duties under control, it is time to plan the balance of the day. Walk the beat. Meet with others involved in community-based initiatives. Appear in court. Schedule times to check back into the office for calls and to confer with volunteers.

Specific Responsibilities

The following recapitulates the most important specific responsibilities of the community policing officer.

- Organize the community and build a sense of pride and ownership.

- Plan and institute community-based problem-solving initiatives.

- Assist young people by:
  — being a positive role model.
  — establishing positive educational/social/athletic activities.
  — providing alternatives to gang membership.
  — offering a more nurturing environment.
  — involving and supporting parents.
  — networking with schools and other agencies that can help.
  — identifying and dealing with child abuse.

- Work with special groups, ranging from juveniles, women, and the elderly, to the homeless, runaways, and substance abusers.

- Gather information with others in the department.

- Network with other agencies that can help, and document contact for others in the department.

The Neighborhood Network Center

As the last example above (networking with others) suggests, community policing officers cannot be all things to all people or they will never have time for their law enforcement duties. The Neighborhood Network Center concept evolved from community policing as a means of attracting other service providers to join the community policing officer in working together to address problems with multi-problem individuals and families.

The Neighborhood Network Center concept seeks to apply the decentralized and personalized model of community policing to the delivery of other public and private social services. This new approach allows other social service providers, such as social workers, public health nurses, mental health professionals, drug treatment counselors, education specialists, and probation and parole officers to join the community policing officer in the community on a part-time and full-time basis. This new community-based team of professionals operates from a facility located in the target neighborhood. Neighborhood volunteers are also an important component. Their help can range from baby-sitting for the teenage mother while she finishes her high school education to helping tutor kids who are having trouble in school.

The community policing officer serves as the informal leader of this new group of community-based problem solvers for many reasons. First, the community policing officer knows the community intimately—its strengths and weaknesses. Second, the community policing officer has already established a bond of trust with the law-abiding people in the community, which can serve as a foundation for the other service providers. Third, the community policing officer acts as the protector for the other professionals who follow his or her lead back into the community, just as the community policing officer is the protector of the private citizens and volunteers in the beat area. Fourth, the community policing officer has the broadest range of options, ranging from a pat on the back for a job well done to the use of deadly force in dealing with the problems that the community may face.

Lansing, Michigan has established one Neighborhood Network Center and plans another. Communities like Newport, Rhode Island; Norfolk, Virginia; and Fort Pierce, Florida are also experimenting with similar efforts.

In Lansing, the impetus began when Community Policing Officer Don Christy talked with a woman who revealed that her alcoholic husband beat her; her son, a high school dropout, was probably selling drugs; and her daughter was pregnant. Faced with such a litany of problems, many community policing officers feel overwhelmed, especially when they realize that there is no system in place that requires agencies to work together or even to take the lead. But in this case, when Officer Christy took his concerns to his department, they provided the leadership necessary to bring agencies together to establish a Neighborhood Network Center in donated office space in Christy's beat.

The idea seems to benefit everyone involved. The community receives a wider range of decentralized and personalized service from one location. This "one-stop-shopping" approach allows multi-problem individuals and families to receive the help they need without running around town from agency to agency, a particular concern in low-income neighborhoods where transportation is often a problem.

The agencies involved benefit by delivering superior service and by re-establishing direct contact with clients. The police officers benefit by being able to refer people to skilled professionals that they know and trust, freeing more time for law enforcement. The police administration benefits because the officer is spending more time on law enforcement duties, and critics of community policing can no longer claim that the job requires police officers to be just social workers.

Space precludes listing all of the agencies that currently operate from Lansing's Neighborhood Network Center, but it should be noted that it provides space for a decentralized police investigator and the regular patrol officers (called "district" officers) who work the three shifts on a 24-hour basis. Working from the same facility has allowed them to become involved in the community-based, problem-solving process and, eventually, Officer Cristy should put himself "out of business" because the district officers will be the community policing officers. Obviously this is a long-term ideal.

For those considering a Neighborhood Network Center, this reform requires:

- A commitment to structural and organizational change within the participating agencies.

- A formal mission statement and letter of agreement.

- A response tailored to local needs and resources.

- Clear support from the top of each participating agency.

- The delegation of authority and responsibility to line-level employees.

- The establishment of a community-based facility in a defined beat area.

- Opportunities for part-time and full-time, line-level employees (and volunteers) to have sustained, face-to-face contact with the community.

- Community input in identifying and prioritizing problems (through surveys and direct contact).

- A focus on problem solving, through a team approach.

- A commitment to recruit and involve local volunteers.

- A mandate to be creative and innovative.

There are still some issues and obstacles to identify and deal with, most notably: funding, how to evaluate success, who will be the leader(s), formal and informal accountability, liability, confidentiality, terminology, and ethical considerations.

There is not yet enough experience with the Neighborhood Network Center approach to identify all of the potential problems that may arise. Among the many questions to be answered are: Will all team members be allowed the flexibility to work hours as needed? How will each agency handle issues of overtime? Is it likely that some team members will shift from part time to full time and back again, as needed? Will team members have the right to change the boundaries of the "beat" area that they serve? As the community stabilizes, for example, we might expect the size of the community policing officer's beat to grow. Will changing demographics in the community require changes in the roster of the team? Will some initiatives be so successful that some team members are no longer needed? If so, does it really make better sense to have them return to working out of a centralized facility? Or should this be the model for the delivery of service, regardless of the level of problems in the community? These and many other questions need to be addressed through ongoing research and evaluation of Neighborhood Network Centers if they are to become the model for high-crime areas. The National Center for Community Policing is currently conducting this research.

Selection of Community Policing Officers

It may take a different type of officer to succeed in community policing, although most contemporary officers can probably succeed if they are given support and rewards. If community policing is to become the way that all police officers deliver service to the community, then everyone in the department should be ready and willing to step into that role.

Some departments have been restructuring their recruiting so that they will attract candidates oriented to the community policing philosophy. In one case, a department produced an introductory brochure that includes information on community policing given to all who apply, and the entrance examination and pre-employment oral interview focuses on the principles and concepts of community policing. As a result, those who do not endorse these ideas typically seek work elsewhere, and interviewers can also screen out candidates who do not seem suited to community policing.

Rookies versus Veterans

There is no formal research to show whether experience in police work correlates with success as a community policing officer, and there are success stories of eager rookies as well as burned-out veterans who claim to be "born again" as community policing officers. Yet there are obvious plusses and minuses that should be considered with both groups.

In the case of rookies and inexperienced officers, the good news is that they have no bad habits to undo and no preconceived notions about the job. Yet, as a general rule, it seems that officers need at least three years of experience to become comfortable with police work. Prior to that, officers often have difficulty in four areas.

- **Making Arrests.** It can be difficult for inexperienced officers to get a handle on the job of making arrests. Some make too many arrests, particularly in situations where other alternatives might make better sense. Others are clumsy or uncomfortable at first. It can take time for many inexperienced officers to get a feel for this aspect of the job.

- **Culture Shock.** Many police officers come from middle-class backgrounds, and they may never have seen what life is like in high-crime, low-income neighborhoods. Problems such as child abuse and domestic assault may be so far from their experience that it will take time for them to learn how to handle such situations.

- **"Red Light and Siren Syndrome."** Many candidates grew up watching police on TV, so they selected police work because it seems to offer action and excitement. As a result, the job can seem dull in comparison. It may take a few years for them to get the desire for action and danger out of their systems.

- **Lack of Knowledge/Information.** Community policing officers network with a host of other government officials and representatives from various agencies, and many young people do not clearly understand how various elements of the "the system" work. While training can address some of these concerns, experience is often the best teacher.

On the other hand, veterans who are jaded or cynical may not find a new lease on life as community policing officers. Some may have succumbed to the negative pressure of peers to the point where their ingrained attitude about the department and about the public would make it hard for them to succeed in a job that requires reaching out to people to establish trust. Others may disagree with the philosophy to the point that nothing can change their minds. Keep in mind that officers who do a great job as traditional police officers may not be good community policing officers, because the job requires different, additional skills.

Selection Criteria

The following is a list of selection criteria that one department uses for the job of community policing officer.

- The expression of interest and qualifications for the position.

- The ability/willingness to physically withstand the rigors of walking throughout the assigned neighborhood.

- The willingness to work flexible hours as community needs dictate.

- The ability to communicate effectively with all levels within the department and with the general public.

- A previous work history that demonstrates dependability.

- The ability to work independently with a minimum of direct supervision.

- Written communication skills, demonstrated via a one-page original document as directed.

- An interest in the position and the ability to communicate effectively, as demonstrated in front of an oral interview board.

Conclusion

This section has attempted to present in as much detail as possible what officers actually do on the job. It must be kept in mind, however, that these are general guidelines and that there will be variations depending on the jurisdiction and the problems identified.

Questions and Answers

What are some of the first things that should be done by a department that is contemplating community policing? First, educate everyone from the top down, including civilians. Next, secure input from the citizens regarding what their problems are, possible office location, and role of the officer. Third, establish a specific job description and role definition for the officer. Before the officer is actually placed in the beat area, he or she should be given some time, a week or two, just to observe the community and to build upon any information about the strengths and weaknesses of the community.

What are some of the first things community policing officers should do when they begin? One of the first things, obviously, is for the officer to understand the beat area, identifying strengths and weaknesses. The officer should take time to drive around and become familiar with the roads, the businesses, the churches, and the neighborhood in general. Then the officer should go door to door, to meet as many of residents as possible, with a letter explaining what the community policing officer's role is. These letters can also be posted in businesses and on bulletin boards, and the media can help. Officers can also attend business meetings, civic meetings, and spread the word that they are in the community, giving the location of the office and office hours. Officers should do everything possible to get the word out that they are there to help identify and solve problems.

How should the beat be selected? The selection of the beat depends on many factors, ranging from the amount of crime and disorder in the area to the density of population, the number of juveniles, and the amount of community organization that exists. Obviously, density of population is a major consideration, because an officer will have difficulty walking in an area that is sparsely populated. Within a 6- to 8-month period, the officer should be able to visit every household in the area, talking to residents or leaving them a calling card or flyer explaining his or her role. If the officer cannot literally knock on every door in that time, the beat is too large. Remember that the officer will be doing much more than just walking and knocking on doors. He or she will be responding to complaints, organizing the community, and performing other job functions. As a rule of thumb, err on the side of making the beat too small. Once the officer gets the beat under control, with citizens' help, it can then be expanded.

Where should the decentralized office be? It does not really matter where it is—a school, a church, a business, or an apartment house—as long as the officer is accessible to the community and does not become co-opted by any particular group: school officials, business people, or other special interests. It is useful to have neighborhood residents volunteer to answer telephones and perform other necessary activities. If the office is large enough, it can become a place where citizens interact with both the officer and other residents.

How does a small department that only has two or three cars out at a time maintain beat integrity when cars answer calls all over the jurisdiction? What departments do in this case is assign a particular area of the city to the officer. He or she will be expected to handle calls all over the city if the other cars are busy, but, on free patrol time, he or she will go back to the assigned area, get out of the automobile, and develop the rapport and the relationships necessary to make community policing effective.

Why do officers enlist the community in activities such as community cleanups, painting, and flower planting that enhance the beauty of the community? If this question is raised by regular officers, supervisors can say, "Why don't you talk to the people you are arresting: the drug dealers, the buyers, and the prostitutes and the disorderly people, and ask them why they ply their trade in particular areas?" Predictably, these officers will find that these persons ply their trade in areas that are disorderly, unkempt, and look disorganized, which acts like a magnet for predators. That is why cleanup is such an important aspect of community policing. Once a community looks like it has pride, then predators are less likely to perpetrate their deviant behavior there. The point of this discussion is also that when questions arise, turn them back on the questioners so they find their own answers. The community policing officer and supervisor should not have to feel the pressure to answer all of the questions, often becoming defensive and abrupt in the process.

Will there be displacement of crime with community policing? The answer is yes, there will be some displacement—for example when drug dealers are pushed out of one area into another. But if that area becomes vigilant and citizens are involved with the police, the constant moving around of the drug dealers may ultimately either convince them to quit selling drugs or to seek treatment if they are addicts. The long-term solution is to have all neighborhoods become active so that there is no place for the "deviant" people to hide.

Should there be "community-oriented public service," not just community policing? The Neighborhood Network Center concept is an example of decentralizing and personalizing other public services. Bringing services closer to the people will enhance delivery and increase accountability.

Does the community policing officer answer radio calls? The community policing officer is a full-service police officer and should therefore answer radio calls. Community policing officers can even provide backup on serious calls if they are in the area. One of the negatives of answering calls, however, is that the officer may get bogged down and just begin reacting and not doing the organizing and preventive work necessary to make community policing effective. If this happens, the officer can be relieved at certain times or hours of the shift to work on identifying a certain problem and solving it. Ideally, the officer should be able to react to calls intermittently. After the officer has developed a rapport with the community, citizens will be patient and often will wait for a response if the officer cannot get there right away. Even if the officer is off duty, citizens will often wait to discuss particular problems with their community policing officer. There should be a balance, but the officer should always take some calls.

If the residents of the area move frequently, can community policing be effective? The more stable the population, the more the residents have a "stake" in the community. The existence of transient populations should not be an excuse not to implement community policing, however. It may be more difficult, but there are always stable elements in any community (businesses, churches, etc.) In addition, whether the citizens are permanent, semi-permanent or transient, they all have a concern for their safety, and that can be the focus for community involvement.

What is an example of an innovative community policing technique? Some community policing officers keep track of deaths in their beat area. When the funeral and visitation times are identified, the officer can make an extra effort to patrol the residences of people who will be attending, denying those who search obituaries for potential victims the opportunity for burglary. Officers can merely leave a calling card in the door to say that they were there, protecting the citizens' property. Obviously this sends a positive message about the police department and the officer, and it may prevent a burglary. Officers on all shifts can participate in this kind of activity.

How can the community policing orientation be applied to a traffic problem? Traffic is a concern, not only because people drive too fast but because of problems like drunk driving. The conventional approach is usually to issue a citation or make an arrest. A community policing approach may include giving speeders a warning and a confidential survey, asking them how the area could be made safer, and how they can be encouraged to slow down. They can tell why they disobeyed the laws, and then give input to help solve the problem. In one community, the problem was that all of the recreational facilities were closed between 3:00 p.m. and 6:00 p.m. for maintenance. Once these hours were altered and most of the facilities were opened, the erratic driving was reduced because the high school students were now using the facilities.

Are barricades and other obstacles effective in supplementing community policing? Barricades and other gimmicks and gadgets are, by themselves, a short-term solution, but can be useful as part of an overall community policing plan. They can give the citizens a false sense of security, transmitting that there are "quick fix" solutions to serious crime problems. In addition, barricades merely push the problem from one area to another, sending the message to predators that they are winning and that their behavior has greatly inconvenienced law-abiding citizens. The cause of the problem needs to be dealt with, not just the symptoms.

How does community policing address graffiti, and what can be done to deal with it? Graffiti is a symptom of problems in the neighborhoods, even if it is not gang related. If the young people have the time and the energy for graffiti, that time and energy can be channeled into constructive purposes. Some courts require that probationers perform cleanup projects and paint over graffiti. However, it needs to go beyond that, and activities need to be developed to help the young people be constructive and learn long-term skills. Recreation activities like leaving high school gyms open at odd hours and using volunteers to supervise the activities are examples of helping young people use their time constructively. Also, art classes and contests can be started to channel their graffiti "talents" into positive directions. There needs to be not only enforcement but also self-enriching activities.

Has the use of cameras and video cameras been successful in combating drug problems in the neighborhood? The use of cameras where citizens mobilize to take pictures of, for example, the license plate numbers of drug customers has been useful as one method of discouraging drug dealing. This, however, is limited to buyers who live outside of the neighborhood. This is not as successful with local drug buyers because they walk to the transaction. With these offenders, there needs to be enforcement, treatment, and prevention.

How do you deal with landlords who continue to rent to drug dealers? Some cities have code enforcement laws that allow boarding up the house if there has been more than one drug raid on the house in a specified period of time. In some community policing efforts where the landlord cooperates with police, the community policing officer can be present when potential renters view the apartment. The presence and the "tact" of the community policing officer can discourage drug dealers from renting. Also, the law-abiding landlords and the community policing officers citywide can have a coordinated communication effort to make sure that drug dealers do not just move from one area of the city to another.

How can a community policing officer deal with stalking? The conventional way to deal with stalking is either to use surveillance or, if the stalker is using the telephone, to put a "tap" on the telephone. In community policing, there would be more community involvement. Neighbors would be made aware of the problem; they would be on the lookout for the stalker. If the victim gets a disturbing phone call, a concerned neighbor could be called to provide comfort. The community policing officer, after having identified this particular problem, may use some surveillance in the traditional police sense but he or she will more actively involve the community.

Can officers who work the night shift be involved in community policing? They can be both a direct and indirect resource for community policing. Directly, they can get to know the neighborhood and its problems. For example, they may leave their calling card at 3 a.m. if they find a garage door left open. A note on the card can caution residents about theft and that they should keep their doors closed. Indirectly, they can use their "dead" time to help the afternoon and day shifts come up with creative solutions to problems that are occurring in the beat area. The night shift often has more "quiet time" to think.

Why is the police officer the leader of the community-based team of service providers? Basically because no other profession is providing leadership. Also, the police officer, with the help of the citizens, needs to make the area safe so that the other service providers will be safe and comfortable working in the neighborhood. In addition, the police officer has the most intimate knowledge of the strengths and weaknesses of the area, and he or she has the widest range of alternatives, from a pat on the back to the use of deadly force.

Is confidentiality a problem when several different professionals are interacting together in a setting like a Neighborhood Network Center? It does not need to be a problem because there is always much "give and take" informally between professionals. The problem arises when the best interests of the client and the community are not considered. The same rules of professionalism and respect for rights should guide behavior in the Neighborhood Network Center as in any professional setting.

Is community policing practiced in all areas, regardless of population? In heavily populated areas, the officer can interact with a large number of people in a limited space. However, if the population is spread out, the officer can go where people congregate, such as athletic events, church functions, and business meetings, to name a few. As long as the officer has enough time, he or she can adjust to population density. Community policing is especially effective in high-crime areas.

After "cleaning up" a drug area how do you keep it from going back to the way it was? The police can "take the beach" but the citizens of the neighborhood have to "keep the beach." The community has to be vigilant (not vigilantes) to make sure the neighborhood stays clean. Citizens need to be continually involved, observant, and doing volunteer work—keeping the lines of communication open with their police department and other agencies in the community.

Is working with juveniles an important element of community policing? Community policing is full-service policing, both reacting to crime and working to prevent it. Prevention means that potential criminals will need to be discouraged from engaging in deviant behavior. Prevention efforts need to focus on young people. Therefore, working with young people is an important element of community policing.

How important is the media? The media can educate the community about community policing: what the role of the officer is, the role of citizens, why people must be patient, and the fact that community policing is a long-term endeavor. Citizens may have to put up with longer response time in nonlife-threatening situations, for example, because officers are taking more time to identify problems and develop long-term solutions. Citizens may have to do more for themselves, so that the officer's free patrol time can be used to deal with long-term problems. The media can help inform the public and can write positive stories on what is happening in the community.

Will the media be receptive to doing positive stories about the accomplishments of community policing? They will do positive stories, but they often do not know what is happening unless you tell them.

Should officers be allowed to talk to the media? Some police departments are reluctant to have officers talk to the media, arguing that they may jeopardize a particular criminal case. Most police administrators can be convinced, however, that the community policing officer can talk to the media about what is happening in the community and what the community is doing to solve problems. A part of the officer's role should be dealing with the media and developing useful information for community newsletters.

Should community policing officers attend separate roll calls? Community policing officers may not always start and end their shifts at the same time as other officers, so it may be difficult to have a common roll call. When possible, however, they should attend regular roll call so that they can be seen and, most importantly, so that they can share information and exchange ideas, and involve the regular officers in solutions to problems. The more interaction that takes place between community policing officers and regular officers the better.

Do community policing officers work all shifts? The community policing officer works 40 hours a week, but the beat is covered by the regular patrol officer 24 hours a day. Because community policing needs to reflect the strengths and weaknesses of the neighborhood, the community policing officer may work any shift or overlapping hours of two shifts. Ultimately, however, all officers should be community policing officers.

Supervising and Evaluating Community Policing Officers

A New Kind of Management

The simplest definition of management is that it involves getting the work done through other people. As pointed out in the previous sections, community policing redefines the nature of the work, from a traditional approach which gauges success by counting calls answered, arrests made, tickets issued, and so on, to one that emphasizes outcomes and solving problems on a long-term basis. By changing the definition of the work, community policing therefore changes the role of police managers.

A paramilitary, authoritarian model of management, which focuses on control, makes sense for the traditional approach. In that system, management alone decides the department's mission and dictates the strategies and tactics that will be used to achieve stated goals. Moreover, management sets forth and enforces the policies and procedures that describe how the work will be done by those below them in the hierarchy. As this suggests, managers are judged on the basis of how well their employees follow the rules and whether the manager succeeds in improving productivity—defined primarily as answering more calls and making more arrests.

Community policing questions some basic assumptions of the traditional system. Primary among them is whether answering more calls or making more arrests translates into making people feel safer and improving the overall quality of life in the community. If the problem is a serial killer on the loose, then arresting the right person solves the problem, since everyone can heave a sigh of relief that the murderer is no longer free to prowl the streets. But if the problem is that low-level drug dealers are causing chaos in the community, mass arrests do not solve the problem if those dealers are simply back on the street within hours, working even harder to make up for lost time. Community policing looks beyond the mere quantification of police activity to see whether the action taken solves the problem from the community's perspective.

Redefining "ends" therefore requires reexamining "means." If the goal is to encourage creative, community-based problem solving, an authoritarian management system that emphasizes control can stifle the freedom and autonomy required to generate imaginative solutions. Rigid policies and procedures that spell out every aspect of how a job is to be done puts employees in a straitjacket that can inhibit them from taking risks on new ideas. A shift to community policing therefore requires a new management approach based on empowering employees, with managers as facilitators whose job becomes finding ways to help them do their best.

This holds true for all police managers and supervisors, from the chief to the sergeant. By transferring decisionmaking from the top to the bottom of the police pyramid, community policing shifts the emphasis from issuing orders and demanding compliance to leading by example, inspiring others to do their best, providing them the tools and assistance that they need, and then getting out of their way so that they can do the job—supplying encouragement, guidance, and advice as necessary.

The Perspective of the First-Line Supervisor

To aid you in understanding how this management style works, this section will discuss the issues from the perspective of the first-line supervisor, since experience shows that it is often sergeants who make or break community policing. If that sounds like an overstatement, consider the importance of the sergeant's role, which is to translate management's missions and goals into action on the street. Then consider how many times we have heard sergeants say, "I have seen fads come and go. I have outlasted several chiefs, all with their own new ideas. What makes you think I can't outlast this one, too?"

Sources of Resistance

The point is not that sergeants are all naysayers and cynics, eager to sabotage any new idea that comes their way—though there are always some in any group who will simply resist any change outright. Much of the most serious resistance to community policing comes from those who see the change as a rejection of their life's work. Many sergeants joined the force when doing a good job was clearly defined as "catching the bad guys," and many put their lives on the line to do just that. So if enthusiasts introduce community policing in ways that imply a total rejection of the past, they are setting up a situation where veterans will balk.

Any change implies a break with what has gone before it. But community policing includes maintaining the ability to intervene decisively in emergencies, which means that officers will always put their lives at risk. The difference is that community policing proposes making better use of non-emergency time, involving officers in proactive, community-based problem solving that holds the promise of paying off not just today but tomorrow.

Some sergeants also fear hitching their careers to a bandwagon that can leave them stranded if the chief leaves. Others recognize that community policing asks them to make an emotional investment in this new approach, and they resist doing so until or unless they are sure the reform will last.

Resistance also comes from sergeants who believe that their job is tough enough as it is and who worry that community policing will make it even tougher, asking, "How am I supposed to keep an eye on those new community policing officers out there doing who knows what?" and "If totalling up calls answered and arrests made isn't enough, how am I supposed to assess their performance?" Part of the answer to both questions is, of course, that sergeants who supervise the community policing officers must get out there and walk the beat with their officers, and some find this unsettling. Sergeants often feel that they will be losing power and authority that they have worked hard to obtain. They need to understand that even though their "power and authority" may be somewhat diminished in the traditional sense, their responsibilities will increase and they will have greater latitude to make decisions and influence policies and procedures.

What Sergeants Want

While some concerns listed above can be addressed through training—and some griping should simply be disregarded—the importance of building support for community policing among first-line supervisors cannot be ignored. In talking with sergeants from around the country who are trying to make community policing work, we have gathered a list of their concerns. One of their primary complaints stems from the feeling that, "Community policing expects the officer to cater to the community, and it expects me to cater to them, but no one caters to me." Many feel that they have not been part of the planning process, have had little influence in implementation, and are expected to continue demanding the same production from their officers as in the traditional approach. The following is a "wish" list that they believe would help them succeed in their jobs.

More authority.	Relief from paperwork.
Clearer role definition.	More resources.
More feedback, understanding, and backing from administration.	More recognition for contribution and "less scapegoating."
More input into policymaking and decisionmaking.	Insight into the "big picture" behind administrative decisions.
More training; more in-service schools.	More independence.

As you will see, many of these themes appear in the following analysis of the basics of first-line supervision in a community policing department. We have divided the material into internal and external functions.

Internal Functions*

Support from the Administration

Successful implementation of community policing as a department-wide change depends on strong leadership from the top. The chief and top command can demonstrate their support to first-line supervisions by:

- Practicing community policing internally by involving everyone in the department, especially first-line supervisors, in the planning process as soon as possible.

- Treating first-line supervisors as a valuable source of information, ideas, and experience.

- Providing clear and concise job descriptions for both community policing officers and their first-line supervisors.

- Avoiding the temptation to use the community policing officer position as a dumping ground for problem employees.

- Backing first-line supervisors who make well-intentioned mistakes.

- Shielding first-line supervisors from political interference.

Inter-Unit Interaction

The goal is to make sure that the entire department functions as a team. First-line supervisors play an important role in this effort by:

- Explaining the role and function of community policing to others in a positive light.

- Integrating community policing officers with other units, most importantly with motor patrol. Accomplishing this can require:

  — Emphasizing that community policing officers obtain information because of their close relationship with citizens that is useful for others, especially investigators.

  — Increasing opportunities for motor patrol and community policing officers to interact, formally (roll call, meetings) and informally (coffee breaks, lunch, and other social gatherings). One department encourages community policing officers to "take a motor officer to lunch."

  — Providing opportunities for representatives from both groups to exchange jobs for a few days or weeks.

  — Structuring situations where others (motor officers and investigators) can work together on community-based problem-solving initiatives.

---

* Sergeant Andrew George of the Lansing Police Department contributed to this section.

— Emphasizing community policing's successes, especially by emphasizing the ways that community policing officers help to make other people's jobs easier and safer.

— Mediating disputes or misunderstandings and challenging those who treat the opposite group with disrespect.

— Giving other units credit for their contribution. (Obviously the best way to integrate motor patrol with community policing is to have them slowly assume community policing functions so that the total patrol division practices community policing.)

• The first-line supervisor can also keep in close contact with other supervisors, even filling in for them on occasions.

Individualizing Supervision

Community policing involves tailoring responses to local needs, which means that each community policing officer may do things a bit differently, necessitating that the supervisor individualize supervision. To understand how the officers are performing, first-line supervisors should:

• Spend as much time as possible in the field communicating with and observing the officers in their beats. (Sergeants often say that they can quickly tell how their officers are doing just by watching how residents respond to them—as a trusted friend or as a stranger.)

• Attend community meetings with the officers.

• Use formal or informal surveys to sample community residents to gather input and information.

• Analyze officers' activities to determine whether they are balancing reactive and proactive initiatives. If community policing officers become reluctant to make any arrests, this is a cause for concern.

• Identify and talk with representatives of other agencies that officers work with.

• See that the officers are advocating for citizens without going to the extreme. (One officer went in uniform with citizens to picket at city hall. This would be considered inappropriate.)

Team Building

To enhance communication and avoid misunderstandings, first-line supervisors should consider:

• Holding weekly meetings so that officers can share information and ideas.

• Writing memos, newsletters and so on, to enhance working together as a team.

- Structuring informal social activities so that officers can get to know each other as people.

- Dealing with personality conflicts.

Supporting the Officers

The first-line supervisor's role as a facilitator includes:

- Treating the officers as respected colleagues with good ideas and instincts.

- Encouraging autonomy and independence by avoiding the temptation to "micromanage."

- Fostering creativity through brainstorming sessions.

- Pitching in and helping on occasion, to demonstrate that the supervisor is not asking anyone to do things that he or she would not do.

- Facilitating opportunities for formal and informal training and cross-fertilization with other departments.

- Cutting red tape, not adding to it.

- Identifying resource people within the community that the officers can turn to for assistance with various initiatives.

- Carrying the message to upper command about the resources that officers need to do the best job.

- Emphasizing officers' triumphs to supervisors whenever possible, giving credit to the officers.

- Promoting risk-taking by public backing of officers who make well-intentioned mistakes.

One example of support involves a community policing officer who was so successful in mobilizing the community to identify and arrest drug dealers that the dealers began to lodge false complaints to the department's Internal Affairs Division. The Assistant Chief, who was not sympathetic to community policing, overreacted to the increased complaints by telling the officer, "I knew community policing would lead to corruption, and I am going to verbally reprimand you and take you out of your beat." The sergeant came to the officer's defense and told the Chief that he was playing right into the drug dealers' hands by removing the officer from the beat—even though the investigation was not complete, early indications were that all of the complaints, most made by convicted drug dealers, were false.

Preventing Burnout

There is stress in any job, but community policing produces a different kind of stress than traditional police work because of the intensity of the personal interaction with people in the community. Many community policing officers have a difficult time saying no to requests, and some become so enthusiastic that they do not want to. As one community policing sergeant said, "My biggest problem is telling my officers to go home and not come back to the beat on their days off and while on vacation. One officer even gave his home telephone number to all of the residents. He never left the job."

First-line supervisors should:

- Talk with officers about the need to maintain balance in their lives.

- Encourage officers to take their allotted time off.

- Be on the lookout for signs that community residents are manipulating the officers into doing things that they should be doing for themselves.

- Encourage officers not to neglect their families, perhaps by suggesting that they invite family members to participate in community events.

- Make sure that officers are not doing the work that other social service agencies should be doing. Discuss strategies with both the officers and your supervisors on how to enlist the direct help of other social service agencies who should do their share.

- Be alert to signs of burnout: fatigue, complaints from spouses, overuse of alcohol, frequent illness or accidents, and so on.

- Where appropriate, urge officers under stress to take advantage of counseling services the department may offer.

- Remember to listen and offer help when the pressures become intense. Officers cannot read minds; they should be told that their supervisors can be turned to for help.

Rewards

The most successful community policing officers tend to be self-starters who derive satisfaction from knowing that they are doing their best to make a difference. That does not mean, however, that they do not want and need a pat on the back for a job well done. Probably the most important rewards the officer receives are the intangibles like compliments from residents and status on the beat. The days of "Your reward is your paycheck" are long gone.

First-line supervisors can also reward good performance by:

- Praising officers, privately and in front of their peers.

- Nominating officers for departmental awards.
  - If community-based problem solving does not qualify under the current awards program, efforts should be taken with superiors to change the rules so that it does.

- Demonstrating trust and support by flexibility.
  - For example, officers who are doing a good job should be allowed to work the flexible schedules they recommend, without needing to provide excessive justification and documentation.

External Functions

As has been stressed throughout this publication, the support of the Big Six (the police, the community, elected civic officials, the business community, other agencies, the media) is essential. The responsibility for bringing them on board rests with both management and line-level personnel, and this means that individuals within the department must interact with representatives of the Big Six, appropriate to their level. In other words, while the chief is the likely candidate to discuss ideas and problems with the mayor, first-line supervisors may find themselves working out the details with various aides.

The Community

Interaction with the community can mean dealing with average citizens as individuals, in groups, and through their leaders. The first-line supervisor's job requires assisting community policing officers in efforts to involve everyone in the police process. Keep in mind, however, that community policing officers often become unofficial leaders in the community, and, while this is an important aspect of the job, it also has the potential to create problems with leaders (and self-appointed leaders) within the community who may view community policing officers as rivals. Part of the first-line supervisor's job is preventing and mediating potential conflicts.

Elected Civic Officials

Unless handled properly, working with elected civic officials can be difficult because the police must maintain their non-partisan status and neutrality while politicians must always focus on winning votes. Community policing depends on the support of elected officials for its very existence, since politicians who become foes may succeed in eliminating it. So it is vital that community policing officers offer elected officials opportunities to participate in initiatives that affect their constituents, not only because their help can be beneficial but also to avoid the concern that community policing officers are building their own competing power base. At the same time, it is the first-line supervisor's job to ensure that the officers are not justifiably perceived as crossing the line into partisan politics.

The Business Community

The business community covers businesses that range from major corporations to "Mom & Pop" stores to private security. The goal of the first-line supervisor is to ensure that community policing officers are meeting the business community's needs and to solicit the business community's support and participation. Again, contact with executives at major corporations will likely be handled by the chief and top command, while the first-line supervisor and community policing officers will probably work with corporate representatives at lower levels. Much of the first-line supervisor's time will be spent working directly with merchant's associations, landlord groups, small-business owners, and so on. First-line supervisors should maintain contact with private security officers, to exchange information and make sure that their roles are not in conflict.

Other Agencies

Community policing officers typically network with a variety of other public and non-profit agencies, ranging from code enforcement and public housing management to homeless shelters. First-line supervisors can help by identifying individuals within various agencies willing to help. They can document those contacts and share them with supervisors of other beats. Effective supervisors make a point of scheduling face-to-face meetings with various groups that can help, and the job includes introducing community policing officers to relevant persons. As discussed earlier, the Neighborhood Network Center concept allows representatives of many agencies to work together from the same office, which greatly facilitates coordinating efforts to intervene with multi-problem individuals and families.

The Media

As noted before, the police often avoid journalists, but community policing produces human interest success stories that can help build public support. First-line supervisors can be an effective link to the media, alerting them to stories of interest and working with them so that they understand how community policing operates. The community policing officer should be the contact person whenever possible.

Other Functions

The discussion of the internal and external functions performed by first-line supervisors only scratches the surface of what they do. Many community policing officers work in public housing through grants provided by the U.S. Department of Housing and Urban Development, which means that first-line supervisors often assist in writing the grants, reports, and evaluations required. There are several sources for grants, ranging from local private foundations to statewide funding agencies. At the federal level, the Bureau of Justice Assistance is a good source. University and college grants offices can provide listings of local, state, and federal grant sources.

First-line supervisors can also have an important role to play in working with the union to provide community policing officers the flexibility that they need to do the best job. Since assessing performance is one of management's most important functions, the balance of this section will focus on that crucial issue.

Performance Evaluations

Adopting community policing department-wide requires modifying everyone's performance evaluations to reflect the philosophy. However, it is the community policing officer out on the beat who most completely and directly expresses the community policing philosophy, so structuring a valid and workable performance evaluation of the community policing officer's job provides the guide for all the other performance evaluations.

Before struggling with the question of how best to assess the performance of the community policing officer, it is important to discuss some of the reasons that performance evaluations are kept. Indeed, many employees resent or ridicule the effort as a waste of time. Others think that management documents performance merely to avoid litigation or defend their decisions in a lawsuit or grievance procedure if someone is fired.

Well-crafted performance evaluations do provide the department with the documentation that they need to justify dismissals. The most basic purpose, however, is to give the employee honest feedback to the question of "How am I doing?"

The problem is that many employee evaluations fall short of accomplishing even these basic goals. All too often, formal evaluations overvalue those who "play the game" by generating the numbers. Indeed, too many performance evaluations penalize those who innovate. As one former police officer noted, officers who do little more than show up on time, neatly dressed, may score better than the creative officer willing to take a risk. The evaluation process in most police departments is "risk averse"—"just don't let us hear any bad or embarrassing news and you will score okay." The winners are those who best play "Cover Your 'Anatomy'."

This kind of performance evaluation process stifles creativity and impairs morale. Admittedly, it is far easier to craft a performance evaluation that measures and rewards busyness, efficiency, and speed rather than effectiveness. So the attempt to create performance evaluations for community policing officers that accurately reflect the virtues of the approach is indeed a challenge. On the one end of the spectrum is the performance evaluation employed in a small department in Texas where the community policing officers are asked to write one or more sentences every few months about what they are trying to accomplish. While that may be enough to satisfy everyone inside and outside the department in a small town where everyone knows each other, consider the challenge of fashioning fair and effective performance evaluations for community policing officers in a department like New York City, which employs almost 30,000 police officers.

The best way to address the challenge of developing a suitable performance evaluation for the community policing officer requires identifying the many objectives that an ideal evaluation would meet:

- To document the individual community policing officer's performance.

- To provide some basis for comparing one community policing officer's performance to another's.

- To serve as a foundation for future goals for the individual community policing officer evaluated.

- To gather and document effective strategies and tactics that can be shared with others.

- To collect and analyze efforts that failed, to warn others of potential pitfalls.

- To contribute data to assessments of the impact and effectiveness of all community policing officers within the department.

- To serve as a foundation for decisions concerning community policing officers, such as those related to training, development, etc.

- To contribute to assessments of the impact and effectiveness of community policing as a department-wide commitment.

- To provide documentation useful to public policymakers/funders.

- To assist the community policing officer in establishing goal-directed activities toward specific problems.

- To help the community policing officer assess, with feedback, his or her progress toward solving neighborhood problems.

Combining the individual community policing officer's evaluation with other material can help make quality a countable commodity. The optimal approach would supplement basic information-gathering with an essay, to capture anecdotes and to flesh out the data. The challenge is to identify quantifiable outcomes that truly relate to the job and yet to ensure that this does not corrupt community policing by trying to turn it into policing by the numbers.

Opening Up the Process

Part of the solution in reassuring people inside the department that the performance evaluations are meaningful and fair requires allowing community policing officers input into the process of developing their own performance measurements. Once they understand the range of purposes that a performance evaluation must meet, they will appreciate the difficulties involved, and supervision will have gone a long way toward allaying their anxiety about its uses. There will always be cynics who will carp at the process, but community policing recognizes the importance of opening up dialogue as a means of enhancing trust. However, for the opportunity to be meaningful, the department must be willing to allow community policing officers to make substantive contributions in developing the measurements by which they will be judged.

It is vital to ensure that the evaluations focus on behavior—not character, not personality—as a means of enhancing objectivity in the process. Every department wants officers to be hardworking, honest, fair, dedicated, brave, compassionate—but the challenge is to find ways to measure the relevant behavior without resorting to subjective judgments. First-line supervisors can tour the area and ask residents for feedback on how often they see the officer, if they know him or her by name, and if the officer has been civil and helpful—focusing on what the officer does, not on who he or she is.

Indeed, many departments have undoubtedly hired individuals who have hidden prejudice toward one group or another. But the issue is not what the person thinks or feels—it is what he or she does on the job, including any misbehavior that must be uncovered and dealt with. If an officer can overcome biases and behave appropriately on the job, difficult as that may be, then personal feelings and attitudes are irrelevant in a performance evaluation.

The other consideration in soliciting support for performance evaluations concerns how they are used. It does not take long for employees in any organization to figure out when the performance evaluations are used for punitive rather than constructive purposes. One function of performance evaluations is indeed to provide documentation to justify disciplinary action, but this use should apply to only a handful of cases.

Performance evaluations are not a bludgeon to whip people into shape, but rather a tool that can be used to set goals for the future. The challenge is to make the officers a real part of the process, so that they do not feel that they are being coerced by supervisors who have no feel for their problems and potential.

Goal Setting and Problem Solving

The real function of the performance evaluation for the community policing officer should be that it provides him or her the structured opportunity to talk with management about how to make even more of the job. Indeed, as one management expert said, the biggest mistake that managers make is to use performance evaluations as a way to dwell on weaknesses rather than to enhance strengths. Managers often use performance evaluations primarily to identify weaknesses, then the hapless employee spends the next few months struggling to improve—often to the detriment of the person's strengths.

Obviously, if the problem is serious (excessive use of force) or easily rectifiable (chronic tardiness), managers must demand immediate, positive change. But consider the department that urged its community policing officers to write a newsletter for their beats. Community Policing Officer Johnson is a superstar on the beat when dealing with people face-to-face but cannot put pen to paper without gritting his teeth in agony. Each time there is a performance evaluation, Johnson is told that he must concentrate on putting out that newsletter—his boss spends more time talking about that than about all of Johnson's wonderful new projects. So instead of concentrating on what he enjoys and does well, Johnson spends hours in the office, struggling to put together a newsletter that is likely to be poor at best.

The solution? Encourage Johnson to find someone else—a citizen volunteer, the local minister, a teacher—to write the newsletter, freeing him to spend more time doing what he does best. In essence, this means applying community policing's personalized, problem-solving approach and the emphasis on organizing resources to the problem of producing a good newsletter.

The danger, of course, is that some may perceive "letting Johnson off the hook" as a serious fairness issue. A fellow community policing officer who spends the time to produce a newsletter may resent seeing Johnson "get away" with "sloughing the job onto someone else." Indeed, because the department will want to document the production of that newsletter, Johnson may even be able to claim credit for it, even though it does not take much of his time.

At a certain level, this is reminiscent of squabbling among kids in a family, but the issue of fairness must be addressed in order to reduce internal friction and maintain morale. And the best explanation is that tailoring the performance evaluation process to the individual, when feasible, will ultimately prove to be the fairest system.

Again, if officers are involved in the process of developing and modifying performance evaluations, they will begin to recognize that they may lose in one instance, but that they can gain in another. Also of importance is the reminder that the goal is to move beyond the family model, where the parent tells the child what to do, to one where adults reason together about how best to proceed—and that requires greater flexibility.

Building an Evaluation

To understand how we can proceed to produce a performance evaluation for community policing officers that includes countable items, it pays to look at the kinds of measures used to assess the performance of the traditional motor patrol officer. While we can debate how well these parameters actually relate to success in the job, the fact remains that most motor patrol officers are evaluated on countable items such as:

Radio Calls. Number and types of calls, alarm responses (true and false); disposition; reports written; time spent; follow-up required.

Arrests. Number and types of felonies and misdemeanors (self-initiated and assigned); warrants; juvenile apprehensions; drunk driving arrests.

Traffic. Number and types of traffic stops (moving and non-moving), including seatbelt and child-restraint violations (self-initiated and assigned); accidents, injuries; citations issued; action taken; time spent; motorist assists; parking tickets issued.

Suspicious Persons/Situations Checked/Investigated. Number and type (self-initiated and assigned); number of persons contacted; action taken; disposition; time spent.

Property Recovered. Type and value, time spent.

Desk/Other Assignments. Number and type, time spent.

Administrative/Miscellaneous. Roll call, court appearances, prisoner transport assignments, subpoenas served, patrol car maintenance, reports written/taken, bar checks, etc.

Community Policing Officer Performance Evaluation

In addition to the items listed above, the performance evaluation for the community policing officer must take into account factors directly and indirectly related to the officer's performance. The following is an initial attempt to contribute to a model.

Outcomes Indirectly Related to Officer Performance.

• *Crime Rates.* Number and types of crimes in beat area; trends up or down from previous month, year; crime analysis.

• *Agency Involvement.* Number and types of other public and private social service agencies operating in the community (including agencies working out of a Neighborhood Network Center).

Statistics for crimes in the community policing officer's beat area are a valid part of any performance evaluation; however, it is important to recognize that this may be only indirectly related to the specific officer's performance. Also, while the participation of other public and private social service agencies in community-based problem solving is a valid goal, the community policing officer may lack the power to make this happen.

Outcomes <u>Directly</u> Related to Officer Performance.

- *Rates of Targeted Crimes.* Number and type; monthly and annual trends. (With input from the community, the community policing officer may have prioritized specific crimes: drug dealing, burglary, vandalism, etc.)

- *Neighborhood Disorder.*

    — *Social Disorder.* Open drug use/sales, panhandlers, runaways, addicts, "winos," truants, curfew violations, prostitution, homeless, mainstreamed mental patients, unlicensed peddlers, gambling, loitering, unsupervised youngsters, youth gangs, etc.

    — *Physical Disorder.* Graffiti, abandoned cars, abandoned buildings, potholes, trash in yards, litter on streets, building code violations (residences and businesses), etc.

The first-line supervisor and the community policing officer can work together to decide which items apply, then they can develop ways to measure progress. Some items will be countable (see below); the community policing officer can tabulate how many abandoned cars are tagged and towed, but the overall perception of improvement in neighborhood decay will require an on-site assessment from the first-line supervisor. If resources are available, the department could also survey residents periodically to assess their perceptions of progress toward improving the safety and quality of life in the beat.

- *Calls for Service.* Number and type; monthly and annual trends.

Experience shows that a new community policing effort typically results in an increase in the number of calls for service from that area, as people begin to look to the police for solutions to problems more than in the past. However, over time, most effective community policing officers discover that the number of calls for service declines as people wait to tell the community policing officer about problems in person, or because residents begin handling more conflicts informally. Monitoring calls for service not only helps verify whether the community policing officer is doing a good job in the beat, but public policymakers should also appreciate that the time saved allows the police to do more with the same resources.

Quantifiable Activities. (Note: There is some redundancy and overlap among categories.)

- *Communications.*

    — *Community Meetings.* How many, what kind, number of people in attendance. Did officer attend, organize, or both?

    — *Newsletters.* Size, frequency, number of readers.

    — *Organizing.* Number and type of block/watch groups formed; monthly and annual trends; number of other kinds of groups and projects formed; number of participants; demographics of participants; time spent.

    — *Telephone Calls.* Number, type, time spent including answering machine messages and dispositions of calls.

— *Speeches.* Number, kind of group, size of audience, time spent.

— *Home and Business Visits.* Number, kind of group, size of audience, time spent.

— *Personal Contacts (on the street, drop-ins at office).* Number, type, time spent.

— *Media Contacts.* News releases, interviews, etc.

— *Other Outreach.* Surveys, feedback from community leaders, etc.

• *Social Disorder.*

— Number and type of group projects aimed at the problems of social disorder listed above; number of people involved; demographics of participants (race, income, etc.); participation of youths, area businesses, public agencies (social services, etc.), non-profit groups (Salvation Army, etc.)

• *Physical Disorder* (beautification).

— Number and type of group projects aimed at the problems of physical disorder listed above; number of people involved; demographics of participants (race, income, etc.); participation of youths, area businesses, public agencies (code enforcement, etc.), non-profit groups (Boy Scouts and Girl Scouts, etc.).

• *Anti-Drug Initiatives.*

— Number and type of individual and group initiatives aimed at drug use (demand); number of people involved; demographics of participants; participation of youths, area businesses, public agencies (drug treatment counselors, etc.), non-profit groups (12-Step Programs, etc.).

— Number and type of individual and group initiatives aimed at low-level drug dealing (supply); number of dope houses closed; number of open drug markets closed; number of arrests; number of people involved; demographics of participants; participation of youths, area businesses, public agencies, non-profit groups.

• *Special Groups* (juveniles, youth gangs, women, the elderly, the disabled, the unemployed, the poor, etc.).

— Number and types of individual and group proactive initiatives aimed at the special needs of fragile, troubled, or uniquely vulnerable groups; number of people involved; demographics of participants; participation of youth, area businesses, public agencies, non-profit groups.

— Note in particular those occasions when the community policing officer provided specific support to families, including single-parent families (individual or group initiatives aimed at individual families or groups of families to reduce problems of domestic violence, child abuse and neglect, etc.).

- *Networking.*

  — Number and types of contacts (in person, telephone, correspondence) with: citizens, community leaders, business owners/managers, corporate officials, other social service or city service providers, agents of non-profit groups, church officials, teachers/educators, print and electronic media, etc. (Note: Using numbers can be useful but their limitations need to be recognized. For example, an officer may abuse numbers by walking by a park and counting all of the children in the park as juvenile contacts.)

- *Referrals.*

  — Number and types of referrals; number and types of agencies involved; number of referrals per agency.

- *Intelligence Gathering/Information Sharing.*

  — Number of occasions when the officer received useful information that contributed to resolving a crime, disorder or drug problem; amount and kinds of useful information generated about a crime, disorder, or drug problem (aliases, street names of drugs, availability of different kinds of drugs, etc.); contribution to crime analysis; number of occasions information was shared with others in the department (name of unit, type of information).

- *Innovation.*

  — Documentable incidents where the community policing officer has demonstrated an imaginative approach toward problem solving— through new projects, new use of technology, etc.

  — List specific proactive initiatives (educational, athletic, and social activities for youth and families, etc.).

- *Teamwork.*

  — If community policing officers work as part of a team with other police officers (motor patrol, narcotics, etc.), the performance evaluation should reflect the number of contacts/joint activities; outcomes; time spent.

  — If the community policing officer is part of a Neighborhood Network Center, document the interaction with other public social service providers who work from the facility. Note separately those occasions when the community policing officer's role was specifically to protect the other social service agents and when the officer was a participant in group problem solving.

- *Solicitation of Resources.*

  — Number and kind of donations from: individuals, foundations, private funders, corporations, small businesses, government agencies, etc. (Options can range from donated paint for a fix-up project to a monetary grant.)

— (Note: Officers should always be discouraged from accepting gratuities. For example, a community policing officer was given a microwave oven as a gesture of appreciation from the community. The supervisor wisely made him give it back.)

- *Other Parameters.*

  — There are also a number of standard measurements of an officer's performance that should be part of the community policing officer's performance profile:

Administrative Duties/Responsibilities.

— Attendance (at roll call, on the beat, at meetings, etc.).

— Promptness (or tardiness).

— Courtesy to the public and to fellow officers.

— Cooperation with others in the department.

— Reports (meets deadlines, completeness, etc.).

Professional Improvement.

— Participation in in-service training.

— Attendance at other training seminars/workshops.

— College course work (number of hours, topics, grades).

— Other efforts toward improvement of knowledge or skills (specify details).

Use of Technology.

— Has the officer demonstrated mastery of the appropriate technology (computer, radio, etc.)?

— Has the officer attended workshops/classes on technology when available?

As noted earlier, in addition to the measurements available through this model, the performance evaluation for community policing officers should also include an opportunity for officers to write a brief essay on successes, such as how they express sensitivity for diversity in the job, or on how they overcome vigilantism and apathy on the part of citizens. Quantifiable assessments measure who, what, where, and when, but the essay format allows delving into the how and why.

The officer should also have the opportunity to affix transcripts or tapes of any media coverage of initiatives in the beat. Community policing officers can also solicit letters of support from local residents.

Opportunities for Understanding

An individual community policing officer's performance evaluation should give a useful snapshot in time of that particular officer's activities. Yet performance evaluations must also contribute to a bigger picture: the effectiveness of community policing officers in the field. Toward that end, top command can begin to collect information, so that a broader picture emerges.

Obviously, because community policing often sparks an explosion in creativity, no one can anticipate all the unique efforts that community policing officers will undertake. For example, community policing officers, many of whom are assigned to low-income areas with a high percentage of renters, spend significant time trying to deal with the disorder problems associated with low-income rentals. The following is the kind of analysis that could be done by combining information from a number of community policing officers' performance evaluations:

Sample Performance Evaluations Analysis Report

Affordable Housing

In the past X months, XX community policing officers have spent more than XX hours dealing with the disorder problems associated with the low-income rental housing in their beats. An immediate sign of success was that such initiatives led directly to the closing of XX dope houses, as well as the arrest of XX suspected dealers.

XX community policing officers also held a series of XX meetings with landlords, instructing them on how to avoid renting to dealers and other undesirables. One community policing officer is even working on developing a database that they can use to warn each other of problem tenants.

XX community policing officers had XX contacts with code officials, so that they could work together to upgrade housing stocks—without triggering gentrification that can put affordable housing out of the reach of the poor. The officers were able to affect improvements in XX homes, and they were able to assist in resolving XX landlord/tenant disputes. Community policing officer X is planning to host a community meeting on the rights and responsibilities of landlords and tenants. The officer has also found a donor who will supply deadbolt locks to those tenants who need them.

Community policing officers had X contacts with city officials about improving the streetlighting, to assist in keeping dealers and prostitutes off the street. The officers also made XX contacts with City Sanitation to improve the timeliness of garbage removal.

As this shows, the individual performance evaluations of community policing officers can provide the raw material for a report geared to a specific issue. Some topics are obvious—efforts aimed at the demand side of drugs, for example—but, since community policing tailors its efforts to local needs, the topics targeted for break out may differ from department to department. For example, some departments may have enough data to justify an entry on public housing, while others may not. In other circumstances, the department may want to keep track of efforts aimed at youths, the homeless, or other special groups. Departments in states like Florida may need to document efforts to protect tourists. The categories listed here are general because no one listing could possibly anticipate all of the possible issues that might be worth tracking.

Blending quantitative and qualitative information in this manner can go a long way toward making the case for community policing within the department as well as to public policymakers. This sample report would make an excellent news release to the media on the department's efforts in providing affordable housing. If there is a suitable site, the release of this information might be a good occasion for a news conference. The department must show reporters that footage and photos of officers standing in front of a huge seizure of drugs, guns, and cash tell only part of the story.

A few tips borrowed from the field of journalism: Remember to go from the general to the specific or the specific to the general as a way of making your point, while maintaining interest. In addition, an opening (or closing) anecdote (culled from the community policing officers' essays) would help humanize the effort and drive home the impact that community policing officers have on the lives of real people.

The First-Line Supervisor

A performance evaluation for the sergeant who assists and supervises the community policing officer must obviously build upon the model provided above. The performance of the first-line supervisor can also be measured on the same list of quantifiable activities listed above in terms of the supervisor's activities in the same regard (communication, contacts, etc.) or in terms of actions that the supervisor takes to facilitate the activities of the community policing officers in that regard (such as securing resources that community policing officers can use). To avoid repetition, those activities will not be reported here. The first-line supervisor will also, of course, be evaluated on traditional measures, just as community policing officers are also evaluated on these measures.

Quantifiable Activities. In addition, the first-line supervisor can be assessed on:

- *Contacts with Community Policing Officers.*

    — Number of face-to-face meetings with community policing officers, time spent.

    — Instances of providing direct support to needs of community policing officers: barriers removed, projects supported/encouraged.

    — Number of suggestions made for innovation/problem solving.

    — Number of trips to the beat (announced and unannounced, with and without the community policing officer in attendance), time spent.

    — Number of "assists" with other groups: citizens, community leaders, community groups, civic officials, public agencies, church officials, teachers/educators, non-profit agencies, the media; outcome; time spent.

- *Career Development of Community Policing Officers.*

  — Number of occasions that supervisor facilitates training opportunities and/or secures resources for training community policing officers.

  — Appropriate maintenance and updating of records on community policing officers.

  — Development/execution of an appropriate reward/recognition program for officers.

  — Efforts to acquire appropriate technology; disposition.

  — Maintenance of technology.

- *Political Issues.*

  — Efforts to shield community policing officers from political pressure/interference.

  — Activities designed to educate politicians about the benefits and trade-offs implicit in community policing.

- *Qualitative Issues.*

  — Does the supervisor juggle rotation/fill-ins so that community policing officers are interrupted as little as possible?

  — Has the supervisor cut red tape for community policing officers?

  — Has the supervisor run interference for community policing officers with critics inside and outside the department?

  — What has the supervisor done to shield community policing officers from local politics?

  — Has the supervisor found ways to determine how well community policing officers express respect for diversity?

  — Has the supervisor investigated complaints/rumors about misbehavior, discourtesy, excessive use of force, unethical behavior?

  — Has the supervisor supported community policing officers when they made well-intentioned mistakes?

  — Does the supervisor act as the community policing officers' ombudsman with top command?

  — Does the supervisor "share glory" with the officers?

  — Is the supervisor alert to the danger of burnout among community policing officers?

  — What steps has the supervisor taken to reduce the stress/workload on community policing officers?

  — What has the supervisor done to enhance the autonomy and flexibility of community policing officers?

— Does the supervisor ignore petty concerns?

— Has the supervisor attempted to tailor performance evaluations to the specific problems in different beats?

Conclusion

The first-line supervisor plays an important role in community policing that often deviates from traditional supervision. The supervisor should not only be in the field a great deal, but supervision must be individualized. There are both internal and external functions that need to be carried out. The success of the effort often hinges upon the quantity and quality of interactions between the supervisor and the officers.

Questions and Answers

Why do police officers resist community policing and, more generally, resist change? The very nature of police work is conservative because police are enforcing the laws as they are, not as they "should be." Because officers see society at its worst, they often become cynical. They often resist change because they are practical realists; that is, they want to see signs of commitment to change from the most important actors, the police command, the social agencies, the citizens, and the political leaders. When they feel there is a long-term commitment from these groups, they will usually be more willing to change themselves.

What is in it for the regular officer while community policing is in the experimental stage? Regular officers will see that the community policing officer has made effective links to the community, and they should see a difference in the residents' attitude when they make calls or responds to complaints in the area. Previously, where there may have been a great deal of hostility in the community, the regular motor officers will see the environment has changed a great deal because of the personalized policing that the community policing officer has provided. Also, the regular officers will see that they are going to get good information from the community policing officer because of the rapport and trust. In fact, in one community where a police car was targeted to be firebombed in an attempt to assassinate specific officers, the community policing officer received information that led to arrests before the assassinations took place. Obviously, examples like this get around the department very quickly, and the officers see that this new rapport and new relationship between the people and their police can have long-term positive effects for both the residents and the officers.

How does an officer deal with "hot calls" if he or she is out of the auto? Being out of the automobile on free patrol time is essential in making community policing an effective, department-wide philosophy. Many departments have a "buddy" system. When the officer is out of the automobile, the adjoining beat officer will respond to hot calls if they occur. The officers can adjust their schedules appropriately and take turns being out of their autos.

Should the union be involved in the planning and implementation of community policing? The union is a critical element in insuring the success of community policing. All relevant groups should be involved, and the union is obviously one of the most important groups. Police unions can be very cooperative when they see the many benefits community policing can bring to their members.

How should the administration deal with unions in community policing? Many times, union contracts prohibit the flexibility needed to effectively have a community policing effort. For example, seniority may dictate who gets to bid on the particular assignment or there may be union limitations to the length of the assignment. This, obviously, prevents choosing the best persons and solicitation of volunteers. If the union contract prohibits certain activities, informal agreements with the union, with trade-offs, can lead to effective community policing efforts. Communication and cooperation form the basis for effective community policing, not only external to the department but internally as well. (See Appendix F for a sample union-management agreement.)

Can't private policing help in dealing with the serious crime problems that exist today? It will take everyone's help to solve crime and disorder. However, if the affluent purchase their safety privately, they may not have the political will to support the public police. In the extreme, there could be the private police for the affluent and the public police for the poor, with the public police going from serious call to serious call, without time for proactive policing.

Recognizing that purchasing private policing is a right of citizens and it is here to stay, what is the solution? Private policing companies need to communicate and cooperate with the public police. They need to be regulated so that they use high standards when hiring their people and providing their service. They also need to have a "stake" in the community and a commitment to all citizens. A safe community is "good business" for everyone.

Should there be a cooperative effort between the community policing officer and private security? Private security is greatly increasing in our country, and community policing officers should keep in close contact with private security officers so that they know what private security is doing. There may even be some cooperative arrangements.

How do you evaluate community policing? It should be evaluated both quantitatively and qualitatively. Statistics like arrest rates, clearance rates, and citations issued are important—but other factors that do not directly relate to crime are also important, like the amount of fear of crime, disorder, satisfaction with the service, and the amount of community involvement. Community policing has been evaluated in many places. The results generally are that fear of crime and disorder decrease and positive relations with lower socioeconomic groups increase. Many of the evaluations also show a decrease in crime.

Do community policing officers have more or fewer complaints against them?
There is no definitive research on the subject. However, community policing
officers should have fewer complaints because they are usually volunteers and
are specifically selected because of a desire to serve the "clients" the best way
possible. In addition, because the officers are personally known to the residents,
they are more identifiable and accountable. If they are not performing in accordance with the job description, it will usually be reported. Thus, there is an
effective system of checks and balances that should lead to fewer complaints.

Is there a higher rate of "burnout" with community policing officers? It is a
different kind of burnout than that experienced by "regular" officers. The "regular" officer is going from call to call with little time to address the basis of the
problem or enjoy the satisfaction of "a job well done." Community policing officers have the stability of the assignment, but the pressure is also on to produce
what they said they were going to do. The stress of being held accountable can
be greater than the stress of handling various calls in an impersonal way.

***Are civilian review boards an effective mechanism to ensure police account-
ability?*** The best form of accountability is input and feedback from the recipients of the service. Often, civilian review boards are comprised of people who
are far removed from the street-level delivery of the service. Many are upper
middle-class people who do not understand the plight and the problems of people living in high-crime areas. However, if there is a lack of confidence in the
operation of the police department's internal affairs unit, then an external review
may be necessary until the confidence builds. This group should be representative of the affected population and may even be large enough so that certain persons could be rotated, depending on the problem and the people involved.

What are some ways to reward community policing officers? There are two
kinds of rewards, personal satisfaction of a job well done and formal organizational awards. In community policing, officers feel good about themselves
because they are solving problems; they are dealing with mostly law-abiding
people; they get pats on the back from residents; and, in some cases, the community even holds events to recognize them. This is probably the best form of
reward. However, the organization can also reward community policing
efforts, all the way from including community policing material in promotions, to having award ceremonies for officers who identify and solve problems in the community. In addition, the administration can give pats on the
back to the officers, approve flexible schedules, give them freedom to be creative, and treat them as professionals.

***Are there examples of close cooperation between community policing officers
and other units of the department?*** There are numerous examples. One that is
noteworthy is when an armed robber holed up in his house and threatened to
keep his family hostage and kill them. The community policing officer for that
area not only helped identify the perpetrator, the officer also knew his behavior
patterns. The officer reported to the patrol division, the investigators, and the
S.W.A.T. team about the robber's proclivity to alcohol, and how he would then

beat up his wife, and the fact that his wife would then retreat to her sister's house with the children. The leader of the S.W.A.T. team called the sister. The wife and children were there, and the wife reported that her husband was "dead drunk," asleep on the couch. The team entered the house and arrested him without injury to anyone. It took the teamwork of all the units, and especially the information provided by the community policing officer. Because of the community policing officer's familiarity with his beat and the people in it, the operation went smoothly.

The Future of Community Policing

The police remain the only social service agency open 24 hours a day, seven days a week, that still makes house calls. As a result, the police are asked to solve problems that range from the loud party next door to the student who opens fire in school, never knowing what the next call for service may bring.

It is our contention that community policing offers fresh ways of dealing with the gamut of problems that the police are asked to handle. In the case of the loud party, community policing encourages neighbors to talk with each other and resolve problems informally, so that they need not constantly turn to the police to deal with situations that they could handle better themselves. In addition, by helping to instill a sense of community, community policing can inspire a renewed sense of caring for others that makes it less likely that people will ignore their neighbors' needs and concerns.

In the case of the student opening fire in school, many would argue that this is the sort of situation that exemplifies the virtues of traditional policing's rapid response. But community policing augments the need to provide an effective and immediate reactive response with opportunities for police to play a proactive role in preventing such violence. By targeting juveniles for special attention, community policing allows community policing officers to target troubled youths who are most likely to explode into violence.

Community policing officers can talk with and listen to a youngster, his peers, his parents, and other adults in the community. Is the entire family in chaos? What kinds of help do they need? Do the child's problems stem from child abuse, drugs, low self-esteem, difficulties in class, gang involvement? By networking with other agencies, from social services to school counseling services to drug treatment facilities, community policing officers offer hope of intervention before the bullets fly—which is the best solution.

Yet this analysis underscores the difficulty of gauging community policing's contribution. How do you count crimes prevented? Moreover, the fact that community policing encourages people to share information with police can mean that crime rates rise, as people begin to trust police enough to tell them about incidents that would otherwise go unreported. Studies show that only about one in three crimes is ever reported to the police—only two in five violent crimes. If the department and the public fall into the trap of relying on crime rates as an indicator of police effectiveness, community policing will suffer, since increased crime reporting can make the situation look worse on paper, at least initially, even as the community is actually becoming safer.

Consider as well that the community policing officer who networks a troubled youngster's alcoholic father to treatment may have succeeded in interrupting a cycle of abuse that has gone on for generations, and which might well have otherwise continued for generations to come. Yet that action counts as only one referral on an activity sheet, and critics allege that such activities offer no proof of community policing's effectiveness.

While we have faith that community policing can make a valid and unique contribution, we are also concerned that many of the dramatic changes that the United States faces are far beyond the capacity of even the most dedicated and creative police agencies to solve alone. Unlike the previous sections of this book, where we have attempted to offer concrete, practical advice on how to implement and sustain community policing, in this final section we will explore the challenges that the police will face as we approach the 21st century.

We will begin by looking at the wrenching economic and social changes taking place, and the concern that grappling with these new challenges means that the coming years will be marked by turmoil. On an optimistic note, we will then look at the positive role that community policing can play in reducing the threat of civil unrest. In conclusion, we will explore some of the questions that community policing must resolve if it is to become the way that all police departments deliver service to their communities. The history of policing is littered with the bones of promising initiatives, such as team policing, that sickened and died. Will community policing be equal to the challenge? As you will see, many of the answers lie with you.

Coping with Change

Faced with the daily challenges of police work, it can be difficult to find time to stand back and reflect on the impact that change has on the nature of the work. In annual training sessions held by the National Center for Community Policing, Bruce Benson, Director of Michigan State University's Department of Public Safety, often uses an exercise that helps us understand the different kind of world that our children face today. He asks participants to think back to their days in high school, then answer questions such as:

— Do you remember being afraid that a classmate might be carrying a gun?

— Did you know where to buy marijuana, cocaine, and LSD?

— Were your parents and the parents of a majority of your friends divorced? Did you and most of your friends grow up with stepparents?

— Did you worry that having sex, even once, might give you a fatal disease for which there is no cure?

— Did you expect that learning to use a computer might be required to get a good job?

While some younger readers may answer "yes" to all these questions, those who are older than 35 or 40, the age group that dominates the ranks of police decisionmakers, rarely answer "yes" to more than one question, if that. Benson offers the quiz to remind police professionals whose policies have a direct impact on people's lives of the importance of community policing's two-way flow of information. Departments that cling to an authoritarian model risk insulating and isolating those at the top from the information that they need to understand our changing reality, whereas community policing helps the entire department stay attuned to the changing needs of real people.

As you read through the succeeding sections on the changing economy, the changing family, and the changing face of America, we ask you to consider the implications. Will the United States succeed in creating enough good jobs at good wages to maintain and expand a thriving middle class? Can we find new ways to support the American family, so that the children who are our future will grow up safe and secure? Will we make the transition to a multi-racial society without turning against each other? And how can community policing help?

The Changing Economy

As the United States struggles to sustain its nervous recovery from recession, there is growing concern that upticks in stock prices and paper profits do not always translate into substantial numbers of good new jobs. In the 1950s, the average rate of unemployment was only 4.5%. In the 1960s, the rate rose only slightly, to 4.7%. Then unemployment jumped to 6.1% in the 1970s, then to 7.2% throughout the 1980s, and there is little hope of improvement for the 1990s (Cloward, 1993). Will this country ever again enjoy the kind of boom experienced after World War II? Can we offer the generation growing up realistic hope that they will fare better than their parents?

In *The Politics of Rich and Poor,* Kevin Phillips (1990), who was President Ronald Reagan's chief political analyst, cites figures that show the United States and other Western democracies are losing ground. Between 1987 and 1988, the U.S. share of the world's gross national product declined 2%, while Japan's share rose by the same percentage. By 1989, the United States had only one person in the top 10 among the world's richest billionaires (the late Sam Walton of Wal-Mart), while Japan had six.

We have yet to fully comprehend what it means to live in a global economy, where corporations operate independent of national boundaries. With or without a North American Free Trade Agreement, trends show that high-paying manufacturing jobs are disappearing in the United States, while most of the new jobs created are in the lower-paying service sector. As authors Donald L. Barlett and James B. Steele (1992) report in *America: What Went Wrong?,* in the 1950s, 33% of all workers were employed in high-paying manufacturing jobs—down to 17% today. In the 1980s, the United States suffered a net loss of 300,000 jobs in manufacturing, and we will likely lose one million more by the year 2000.

Bartlett and Steele (1992) note with alarm that the country is fracturing into a two-tiered society. Even without factoring in accumulated or inherited wealth, the gap between rich and poor is growing. In 1989, the top 4% of U.S. wage earners earned as much as the bottom half of all wage earners, whereas 30 years ago, the top 4% only made as much as the bottom third. A 1990 study (*Tax Rates and Income*) shows that, during the previous decade, the poorest fifth of Americans saw their incomes decline 3%, while their tax rates rose 16%. In contrast, the richest fifth of Americans saw their incomes climb 32%, while their tax rates dropped 5.5%.

The Joint Center for Political and Economic Studies echoes these concerns. While the 1980s provided the longest sustained economic boom in U.S. history, prosperity failed to trickle down far enough. Their 1991 study (*Economic Growth*) showed that roughly twice as many families in the United States qualified as suffering "severe" poverty as compared to families in Canada and Britain, and the United States had six times as many families living in severe poverty as West Germany and Sweden. When the researchers looked at single-parent families, they discovered that 45% of such families in the United States qualified as living in severe poverty, compared to only 8% of such families in Britain, a nation in decline that many Americans think of as suffering problems far more severe than those of the United States.

According to this report, "The U.S. poor are more likely to be working; fewer rely on welfare for long periods; fewer are heavily dependent on government support. Yet more remain poor for long periods of time."

The Changing Family

As that reference to single-parent families reminds us, there is a strong link between marital status and income. The rise of two-income families, coupled with the increase in single heads of households, has had a profound impact on the relative fortunes of each.

In the 1950s, family income typically consisted of the wages and salaries of only one working spouse. In the 1990s, it comes from the combined wages and salaries of a husband and wife, both of whom now work outside the home. "Thus, goods and services that once could be purchased with a single income now require two incomes," according to Bartlett and Steele (1992). In addition to the economic implications, the explosion in families where both parents work has produced a new generation of children, the so-called "latchkey kids," who spend less time with their parents.

On the other side of that coin, subtract that second potential wage earner from a family, either because of divorce or a failure of families to form, and single parents find themselves at even greater economic risk than when one income sufficed to raise a family. In 1988 (the latest year for which complete data were available), 94% of tax returns filed by single heads of households and married persons living separately showed incomes of less than $40,000 (Barlett, 1992).

The reality is that the increase in divorce and out-of-wedlock births means that only one of four children growing up today will likely reach adulthood in an intact, two-parent family. A Census Bureau study (*Study: Fewer Homes,* 1991) showed that there are now an estimated 9.7 million single parents, up 41% from a decade ago. The vast majority (8.4 million) are women, with single mothers running 44% of black households, 23% of Hispanic households, and 10% of white households.

The United States is unique in the world in the number of children having babies. In his book, *The Truly Disadvantaged,* William Julius Wilson (1987) notes that 40% of all out-of-wedlock births in the United States occur among women who are minors. A total of 93 of every 1,000 white teenagers and 186 of every 1,000 black teenagers in this country become pregnant every year. In England and Wales, the pregnancy rate is 45 out of every 1,000; in Canada, 44: France, 43: Sweden, 35: and the Netherland, 14 (Hacker, 1992).

Many point to the explosion in out-of-wedlock births among blacks as at least a partial explanation for their failure to keep pace economically. In 1950, fewer than two out of 10 black children were born to unwed mothers. By 1988, the number had risen to more than six out of ten (Hacker, 1992).

However, in *Two Nations, Black and White, Separate, Hostile, Unequal,* author Andrew Hacker (1992) notes that even if black families had the same mixture of single parents and married couples as white households, "the income ratio for black families would only rise from $580 to $732 [compared to each $1,000 earned by white families]." While "having more men's incomes would help, it would not accomplish very much since black men still make considerably less than white men," writes Hacker (1992). "Moreover, even if more black households had a man in residence, some of the men would be unemployed or removed from the labor force for other reasons."

Among the other reasons that a high percentage of black males are not in the work force in the United States is their extraordinarily high rate of incarceration, in large part the result of huge increases in drug arrests and convictions. One in four black males between the ages of 15 and 30 is currently under some form of correctional custody. As a comparison, South Africa imprisons an average of 681 out of every 100,000 black males, but the rate of incarceration in the United States shows that a staggering 3,370 out of 100,000 black males are behind bars (*The Sentencing Project,* 1993).

Education is clearly part of the key in helping families rise out of poverty, but Hacker (1992) shows that the issue of race also challenges our vision of U.S. society as a meritocracy. On one end of the educational spectrum, black males without a high school diploma earn only $797 a year for every $1,000 earned by their white male counterparts. Despite decades of gains, black males with five years or more of college only earn $771 for each $1,000 received by their white male peers.

The Changing Face of the United States

The introduction of race into the discussion also reminds us that the face of the American family is changing rapidly. Succeeding generations will reflect a rainbow of skin colors, and, if census trends persist, whites will lose majority status by the middle of the next century. In California, for example, 58% of the state's total population is white, but white students are already a minority in the state's schools (Henry, 1990).

Hacker (1992) notes that, while much of the discussion concerning race still focuses on black and white, the fastest growing racial groups in the United States for the past two decades have been Hispanics and Asians, followed by Native Americans and Hawaiians. In addition to legal immigration, estimates suggest that as many as one million illegal immigrants attempt to cross the Mexican border each year, and as many as 3,000 a day succeed in entering the United States (Vito, 1993). In the two decades between 1970 and 1990, the percentage of whites in the U.S. population dropped from 83.3% to 74.2%. Meanwhile, the percentage of blacks rose from 10.9% to 12.5%; Hispanics increased from 4.5% to 9.5%; and those in the category of "Asians and Others" almost tripled, from 1.3% to 3.8%.

The combination of disparities in birth rates among races, as well as the impact of changing patterns of legal and illegal immigration, holds the promise of creating the "beautiful mosaic" that New York City Mayor David Dinkins envisions. However, it would be a mistake to conclude that these changing demographics will easily or automatically result in proportional redistribution of this country's power and wealth. Women have long been the majority in this country, yet they are far from the majority in the halls of Congress or in executive boardrooms, and, despite modest improvements, women still continue to earn substantially less than men.

As Hacker's book (1992) so poignantly illustrates, of all races, blacks continue to face the greatest challenge in overcoming prejudice and discrimination:

> . . . [M]embers of all these 'intermediate' groups [such as Hispanics and Asians] have been allowed to put a visible distance between themselves and black Americans. Put most simply, none of the presumptions of inferiority associated with Africa and slavery are imposed on these other ethnicities. Moreover, . . . second and subsequent generations of Hispanics and Asians are merging into the 'white' category, partly through intermarriage and also by personal achievement and adaption. Indeed, the very fact that this is happening sheds light on the tensions and disparities separating the two major races.

Civil Disturbance

U.S. society today is anxiously attempting to adjust to the accelerating pace of economic and social change. Yet the rising tensions and frictions between various races and classes today also remind us of how much things stay the same. Community policing traces its roots to the early foot patrol experiments in Flint and Newark, which were conceived, in large part, to address concerns about racial unrest. Newark had experienced a bloody riot, and many worried that Flint was on the brink of exploding.

The Kerner Commission, which warned that the United States was fracturing into two societies—one white and rich and the other black and poor, also noted that a majority of the riots in that era resulted from action of the police. While, in a number of those cases, the police action that sparked rioting was routine and legal, the commission reported that strained relations between police and minorities provided the tinder that could allow even the tiniest spark to explode into flames. To solve the problem, the police were urged to increase minority hiring and to improve police-community relations.

In 1993, a year after the horrendous riot in Los Angeles that left more than 50 people dead and roughly $1 billion in property destroyed, a rereading of the Kerner Commission findings makes it clear that many of the dynamics remain the same—with two notable differences. Unlike the past, the riot in Los Angeles was multi-racial, more a matter of socioeconomic class than ethnicity, just as futurist William Tafoya (1990) of the Federal Bureau of Investigation had predicted long before.

Other than the racial composition of the rioters, however, what happened in Los Angeles seemed like the recurrence of a horrible nightmare. While not the immediate spark, it was the beating of Rodney King by four police officers that set the stage, and again the drama was played out against the police department's troubled relationship with minorities. Again, a commission—this time the Christopher Commission—urged the police to improve relations with the community. But this time, instead of limited police-community relations programs, the major change is that the Christopher Commission strongly supported community policing reform.

Among the many ways in which community policing reduces the risk of civil unrest:

- Community policing reduces racial tensions by allowing police and residents to get to know each other on a first-name basis, which fosters mutual trust and understanding.

- Community policing encourages a presumption of goodwill on both sides. Everyone makes mistakes, but past experience shows that riots have often resulted from police actions that were well within guidelines. A presumption of goodwill can allow misunderstandings or misperceptions to be addressed with less danger that such situations will spin out of control.

- Community policing provides mutual accountability by reducing anonymity on both sides. On the one hand, community policing allows officers the opportunity to distinguish between individuals they can trust and those to keep an eye on. Moreover, the fact that officers themselves know that they must be back on the same streets day after day acts as an additional check on their behavior, since community policing allows average citizens to hold their officers directly accountable. The dialogue and interaction fostered by community policing encourages residents to challenge officers directly regarding their concerns about abuse of authority, or to speak to their supervisors, if necessary.

- Community policing targets juveniles for special attention, the group at greatest risk of rioting.

- Community policing provides police the opportunity to gather more and better information about the level of tension and potential for unrest in the community.

- Community policing offers a mechanism for police to track incidents with racial overtones. Federal regulations now require reporting so-called bias incidents; however, it can be difficult for police to capture racial, ethnic, or religious slurs that may occur during the commission of other crimes. In the case of graffiti, for example, the police need to know whether it is meant as an expression of racial hatred, a gang threat, or whether it is merely someone's idea of "art."

- Community policing can help to prepare communities for aggressive anti-drug initiatives by involving residents in decisionmaking concerning tactics.

- Community policing directly addresses the problems of physical and social disorder and neighborhood decay that often plague communities at greatest risk.

- Community policing improves communication, which can help in quelling rumors and defusing threatening situations.

- Community policing can act as an early-warning system—for example, by spotting activities of white supremacists or Skinheads.

- Community policing involves average citizens in community-based, police-supervised solutions—reducing the risk that vigilantes will take the law into their own hands.

- Community policing encourages developing proactive initiatives that offer the promise of enhancing safety and the overall quality of life in the community.

Statistics cannot capture riots prevented. In the early 1980s, Flint foot patrol officers were credited with calming a situation that threatened to erupt into a full-scale riot. They were able to walk into an increasingly unruly mob and recruit people they knew to help them ease tensions, and this kind of story has been repeated time and again in other locations ever since.

Future Challenges

If community policing did nothing more than reduce the risk of civil disturbance, it would be well worth the investment. But community policing does far more. If we look at the violence, drugs, and chaos that plague so many of our urban neighborhoods, it seems fair to say, as many have, that major cities with numerous drive-by shootings are suffering "riots in slow motion," and community policing provides the police with new ways to address the myriad of problems that such communities face.

But will community policing survive and thrive? At this point, there are more questions than answers.

Questions for the Future

- Will police departments embrace community policing as a department-wide philosophy, thereby avoiding a split where community policing officers "make nice," while everyone else conducts business as usual?

- Will police departments adopt community policing as a city-wide strategy, instead of as a special program limited to high-risk neighborhoods and therefore vulnerable to cutbacks and cancellation?

- Will there be critical problem analysis and long-term solutions to problems rather than moving from problem to problem without officer decentralization and permanency?

- Will departments revise their policies—specifically those concerning recruiting, selection, training, performance evaluation, and rewards—to reflect a commitment to the philosophy and practice of community policing?

- Can and will departments find ways to free up patrol time so that officers can engage in proactive, community-based problem solving rather than reacting to problems only after they occur?

- Will citizens do more for themselves and be patient with the trade-offs necessary with community policing, like increased response time for nonlife-threatening situations?

- Will departments succeed in developing new quantitative and qualitative measures that accurately reflect community policing's contribution?

- Will supervisors and top command back the officers who are trying to make a difference by allowing them the freedom to fail and make mistakes?

- Will police unions join with management in changing rules so that officers will enjoy the autonomy and flexibility that they need for effective community-based problem solving?

- If police departments do their part, will the rest of the Big Six (the community, elected civic officials, the business community, other agencies, the media) provide the sustained support that community policing needs?

- Will chiefs be provided the job security that they need to take risks and embrace innovation?

- Will citizens spend at least a few hours a month as volunteers so that community policing can succeed?

- Will we slow and then reverse the trend toward two separate police systems—private security for those who can afford it and public policing increasingly just for the poor?

- Will we allow uncertainty about the future to draw us together so that we work collectively to solve our problems, or will we pull apart and selfishly attempt to protect only ourselves?

Conclusion

For community policing to succeed, everyone must do his or her part. We see many enthusiastic community policing officers acting as positive role models, spending their unpaid leisure time and vacations organizing and hosting activities to make life more enjoyable for the people in their beats. But then we also saw a case where community policing officers volunteered their time to coach kids in a series of athletic games, for which upper command actually paid themselves overtime to attend.

The point is not that community policing depends on or requires unpaid overtime to succeed. Indeed, it must succeed or fail based on the work that the police are paid to do, and internal dissent will grow if performance evaluations and promotions appear to favor only those officers willing to spend unpaid time. The issue is not money but equity and setting the proper example. Top command has a responsibility to demonstrate its commitment to its officers—either everyone gets paid or no one does.

Appeals to altruism often flounder on the rocks of self-interest. "What's in it for me?" "That's a police problem, not my problem." "Why should I want to see my tax dollars going to help 'them'?" "All I care about is keeping me and my family safe." For the police to be perceived as a moral force in the community that sets the tone for others to follow, they must demonstrate their commitment to community policing by their example.

Corny as it may sound, community policing will likely succeed or fail depending on whether we believe that there is an inherent goodness within most people that we can do a better job of tapping and nurturing through institutions such as the police. If we view crime, and therefore criminals, exclusively as an evil to be stamped out or locked away rather than as problems that we must constantly struggle to deal with and prevent, then the cynics among us will succeed in killing community policing. But if instead we recognize that we are all in this together, community policing will provide a new way to help draw us together.

Faith and trust may not persuade public policymakers and researchers as easily as statistics. Yet at its core, community policing asks the chief and other police managers to have faith in their officers, investing them with the power to be creative and to take risks. Community policing asks line officers to have faith in people, inviting them into the process of finding ways to help make their communities better and safer places in which to live and work. Community policing also asks public policymakers, civic officials, taxpayers, the business community, community leaders, and average citizens to have faith in the concept that people working together with police can make a difference.

References

Bartlett, D. & Steele, Jr. (1992). *America: What Went Wrong?* Kansas City: Andrews and McMeel.

Bellah, R., et. al. (1991). *The Good Society.* New York: Alfred A. Knopf.

Cloward, R. & Pivens, F. (1993). "The Fraud of Workfare." *The Nation,* May 24.

"Economic Growth Doesn't Shrink Poverty, Inequality" (1991). *Detroit Free Press.* September 19.

Fay, B. (1984). *Social Theory and Political Practice.* London, UK: George Allen & Unwin Publishers Ltd.

George, A. (1992). *The First Line Supervisor's Perspective of Community Policing: A Participant Observational Study.* Unpublished thesis for master of science degree, Michigan State University, East Lansing, Michigan.

Grimshaw, W. (1990). *Future-vision: An Organizational Strategic Planning System.* Kalamazoo, Michigan: Baker and Barnett Publishers.

Hacker, A. (1992). *Two Nations, Black and White, Separate, Hostile, Unequal.* New York: Charles Scribner's Sons.

Henry, W., III. (1990). "Beyond the Melting Pot." *Time Magazine.*

Hoekwater, G. (1990). *Strategic Planning.* Unpublished paper, Western Michigan University; Kalamazoo, Michigan.

Phillips, K. (1990). *The Politics of Rich and Poor.* New York: Harper Perennial.

Sloan, R., Trojanowicz, R. & Bucqueroux, B. (1993). "Basic Issues in Training: A Foundation for Community Policing." *The Police Chief,* LX(5).

Sower, C. (1957). *Community Involvement.* Glencoe, Illinois: Free Press.

"Study: Few Homes Have Kids, 2 Parents" (1991). *Detroit Free Press.* January 30.

Tafoya, W. (1990). "The Future of Policing." *FBI Law Enforcement Bulletin,* 59(1), pp. 13-17.

"Tax Rates and Income" (1990). Congressional Budget Office. *Detroit Free Press,* February 20.

"The Sentencing Project" (1993). In *Harper's index.*

Trojanowicz, R. & Bucqueroux, B. (1990). *Community Policing: A Contemporary Perspective.* Cincinnati, Ohio: Anderson Publishing Co.

Trojanowicz, R., Bucqueroux, B., McLanus, T. & Sinclair, D. (1992). *The Neighborhood Network Center: Part One.* East Lansing, Michigan: Michigan State University, National Center for Community Policing.

Trojanowicz, S. (1992). *Theory of Community Policing.* Unpublished thesis for master of science degree, Michigan State University, East Lansing, Michigan.

Vito, R. (1993). *CNN Headline News.* May 14.

Wilson, W. (1987). *The Truly Disadvantaged, the Inner City, the Underclass, and Public Policy.* Chicago: University of Chicago.

Comparison of Community Policing to Police-Community Relations

Community Policing	Police-Community Relations
Goal: Solve problems—improved relations with citizens is a welcome by-product.	**Goal:** Change attitudes and project a positive image—improved relations with citizens is a main focus.
Line Function: Regular contact between officers and citizens.	**Staff Function:** Irregular contact between officers and citizens.
A department-wide philosophy and department-wide acceptance.	Isolated acceptance often localized in the PCR unit.
Internal and external influence and respect for officers.	Limited influence and respect for officers.
Well defined role—does both proactive and reactive policing—a full-service officer.	Loose role definition; focus on dealing with problems of strained relations between police and citizens; crime prevention encouraged.
Direct service—same officer takes complaints and gives crime prevention tips.	Indirect service—advice on crime prevention from PCR officer but "regular" officers respond to complaints.
Citizens identify problems and cooperate in setting up the police agenda.	"Blue Ribbon" committees identify the problems and "preach" to police.
Police accountability is ensured by the citizens receiving the service in addition to administrative mechanisms.	Police accountability is ensured by civilian review boards and formal police supervision.
Officer is the leader and catalyst for change in the neighborhood to reduce fear, disorder, decay and crime.	Officer provides consultation on crime issues without having identified beat boundaries or "field responsibilities."
Chief of police is an advocate and sets the tone for the delivery of both law enforcement and social services in the jurisdictions.	Chief of police reacts to only the law enforcement concerns of special interest groups.
Officers educate public about issues (like response time or preventive patrol) and the need to prioritize services.	Officers focus on racial and ethnic tension issues and encourage increased services.
Increased trust between the police officer and citizens because of long-term, regular contact results in an enhanced flow of information to the police.	Cordial relationship between police officer and citizens but often superficial trust with minimum information flow to prevent and solve crime.
Officer is continually accessible in person, by telephone, or in a decentralized office.	Intermittent contact with the public because of city-wide responsibility; contact is made through central headquarters.

Community Policing	Police-Community Relations
Regular visibility in the neighborhood.	Officer seldom seen "on the streets."
Officer is viewed as having a "stake in the community."	Officer is viewed as an "outsider."
Officer is a role model because of regular contact with citizens (especially youth role model).	Citizens do not get to know officer on an intense basis.
Influence is from "the bottom up"—citizens receiving service help set priorities and influence police policy.	Influence is from "the top down"—those who "know best" have input and make decisions.
Meaningful organizational change and departmental restructuring—ranging from officer selection to training, evaluation, and promotion.	Traditional organization stays intact with "new" programs periodically added; no fundamental organizational change.
When intervention is necessary, informal social control is the first choice.	When intervention is necessary, formal means of control is typically the first choice.
Officer encourages citizens to solve many of their own problems and volunteer to assist neighbors.	Citizens are encouraged to volunteer but are told to request and expect more government (including law enforcement) services.
Officer encourages other service providers like animal control, firefighters, and mail carriers to become involved in community problem solving.	Service providers stay in traditional roles.
Officer mobilizes all community resources, including citizens, private and public agencies, and private businesses.	Officers do not have mobilization responsibility because there is no specific beat area for which they are responsible.
Success is determined by the reduction in citizen fear, neighborhood disorder, and crime.	Success is determined by traditional measures—i.e., crime rates and citizen satisfaction with the police.
All officers are sworn personnel.	Most staff members are sworn personnel but some are non-sworn.

COMMUNITY ANALYSIS WORKSHEET
by Roger L. Depue

I. GENERAL INFORMATION

A. Jurisdiction Studied (Name)
    1. Type of Jurisdiction (State, Region, County, Urban, Suburban, Rural)
    2. Size of Jurisdiction (Square Miles)

B. Population
    1. Total   1980 _____ 1990 _____
    2. Breakdown:

Ethnicity: (include number and percentage of total)

	1980		1990	
	Number	Percentage	Number	Percentage
Black				
Caucasian				
Hispanic				
Other				

    3. Distribution of Population for 1990 (Age, Number, Percentage)

Age Group	5-14		15-19		20-24		25-34		35-49		50+	
	Number	Percentage	Number	Percentage	Number	Percentage	Number	Percentage	Number	Percentage	Number	Percentage
Age Group												
Total												
Sex:												
Male												
Female												
Ethnicity:												
Caucasian												
Black												
Hispanic												
Other												

C. Income (Families)

	$0-9,999	$10-19,000	$20-40,000	$40,000 +
Total:	_____	_____	_____	_____

Ethnicity:

Caucasian	_____	_____	_____	_____
Black	_____	_____	_____	_____
Hispanic	_____	_____	_____	_____
Other	_____	_____	_____	_____

D. Education (Persons over 25 years)

	No High School (H.S.)	H.S. 1-3 yrs.	H.S. 4 yrs.	College 1-3 yrs.	College 4 yrs. or more
Total:	_____	_____	_____	_____	_____

Ethnicity:

Caucasian	_____	_____	_____	_____	_____
Black	_____	_____	_____	_____	_____
Hispanic	_____	_____	_____	_____	_____
Other	_____	_____	_____	_____	_____

		1980	1990
1.	Total Student Population	_____	_____
2.	Number of Schools	_____	_____
	a. Elementary schools	_____	_____
	b. High schools	_____	_____
	(1) junior	_____	_____
	(2) senior	_____	_____
	c. Colleges and Universities	_____	_____
	d. Adult Education programs	_____	_____
	e. Other (Vocational, Trade, Etc.)	_____	_____

E. Religion

1. Congregations: _____
2. Number of Places of Worship: Protestant _____   Catholic _____
   Jewish _____   Muslim _____
   Other _____
3. Ministerial Associations (Identify by Name):

F.   Government

    1. General descriptive information

        a. Government form (example: City Manager appointed by an elected Mayor and Council people strong Mayor form)

    2. Law Enforcement Agency

    Rank Structure of Sworn Personnel:

	Number	Education			Average		
		Associate Degrees	Bachelor Degrees	Graduate Degrees	Age	Years in Grade	Years in Service
Patrol Officer Deputy Sheriff	_____	_____	_____	_____	_____	_____	_____
Detective	_____	_____	_____	_____	_____	_____	_____
Sergeant (First Line Supervisors)	_____	_____	_____	_____	_____	_____	_____
Lieutenant	_____	_____	_____	_____	_____	_____	_____
Captain	_____	_____	_____	_____	_____	_____	_____
Inspector/ Commander	_____	_____	_____	_____	_____	_____	_____
Deputy Chief/ Undersheriff	_____	_____	_____	_____	_____	_____	_____

Non-sworn Personnel:

Male	Female	Caucasian	Black	Hispanic	Other

3. Government Revenues

Fiscal Year:	Present Year	1990	1980

  a. Total Government Budget _____ _____ _____

    1) Police Department Budget _____ _____ _____

      Salaries _____ _____ _____

      Equipment/vehicles _____ _____ _____

    2) Manpower Distribution:

      Patrol _____ _____ _____

      Criminal Investigation _____ _____ _____

      Administration _____ _____ _____

      Other _____ _____ _____

  b. Tax Base Information
    1) Tax Sources:

	Industrial Property	Commercial Property	Residential Property	Personal Property Tax
1980	_____	_____	_____	_____
1990	_____	_____	_____	_____
Present	_____	_____	_____	_____

  c. Federal Revenue (present) _____

  d. State Revenue (present) _____

II. ENVIRONMENT OF CRIME

A. Social Conditions frequently associated with community problems including crime and delinquency. (Community Weaknesses)

  1. Mobility of Population

    a. Number of people living in different house since 1980 _____

    b. . . . . . . different county since 1980 _____

    c. . . . . . . different state since 1980 _____

  2. Poverty
    Median

Income	Caucasian	Black	Hispanic	Other
1980	_____	_____	_____	_____
1990	_____	_____	_____	_____

a. Unemployment rates

1) Number and percent unemployed

	Number	Percentage
Caucasian		
Black		
Hispanic		
Other		

2) Number and percent of families receiving public assistance

	Number	Percentage
Caucasian		
Black		
Hispanic		
Other		

b. Substandard housing

1) Number and percent of households lacking some or all plumbing facilities

	Number	Percentage
Caucasian		
Black		
Hispanic		
Other		

c. Blight and decay

1) Density of population: Persons per square mile _____

2) Overcrowding: Persons per residence _____

3. Low Education Levels

a. Median school years completed

Total: _____

Caucasian _____

Black _____

Hispanic _____

b. Males 16 to 21 years not attending school

Total: _____

Caucasian _____

Black _____

Hispanic _____

c. Truancy - High School students with unexcused absences in a school year (or comparable measure).

Total: _____

Caucasian _____

Black _____

Hispanic _____

Other _____

4.   Broken Homes

a. Marriage and divorce rate for <u>county</u> for three time periods (Use number per 1,000 persons.)

	1980	1990	Present Year
Marriages	_____	_____	_____
Divorces	_____	_____	_____

(Information is available from Bureau of Vital Statistics publications on marriage and divorce. Statistics broken down by county.)

b. Single Male Headed Households

	1980	1990
Total:	_____	_____
Caucasian	_____	_____
Black	_____	_____
Hispanic	_____	_____
Other	_____	_____

c. Single Female Headed Households

	1980	1990
Total:	_____	_____
Caucasian	_____	_____
Black	_____	_____
Hispanic	_____	_____
Other	_____	_____

5.   Citizen Apathy

a. Persons of voter age and eligibility _____

b. Persons registered to vote _____

c. Persons who voted in past chief executive election:

National	State	City/County
_____	_____	_____

(Information must come from local jurisdiction)

6.   Recidivism Rate
a. Repeat Felony Offenders Arrested
1980 _____
1990 _____
Present year _____

7.   Victimization (Felonious Crimes)
a. Victimization Rate for Crimes Reported to Police
1)   Total victims _____
a) Violent Crimes _____
b) Property Crimes _____

8.   Witnesses Failing to Appear in Court
1980 _____
1990 _____
Present Year _____

III. COMMUNITY RESOURCES AVAILABLE TO COMBAT NEGATIVE SOCIAL CONDITIONS

(Community Strengths)

A. Mass Media

1. Identity of network television stations
2. Identity of independent/educational television stations
3. Identity of radio stations
4. Identity of newspapers
   a. Frequency of circulation
   b. Number of readers

B. Community Organizations - General
(Number and Kind)

1. Professional
2. Unemployment compensation
3. Workers compensation
4. Youth services
5. Community chests
6. Private charitable organizations
7. Day care centers
8. Other

C. Agencies to Assist the Poor and Unemployed

1. Welfare and social services
2. Unemployment compensation
3. Workers compensation
4. Youth services
5. Community chests
6. Private charitable organizations
7. Day care centers
8. Other

D. Education Services

1. School counseling services
2. Parent-teacher associations
3. Child guidance clinics
4. Volunteer organizations
5. Attendance officers
6. Adult education programs
7. Other

E. Recreational Services

1. Department of Parks and Recreation
2. School programs
3. Neighborhood programs
4. YMCA, YWCA, etc.
5. Community athletic programs
6. Civic club competitions
7. Business sponsored competitions
8. Summer camps
9. Police Athletic League

F. Family Assistance Agencies

1. Family courts
2. Counseling clinics
3. Social services
4. Churches
5. Big Brother/Sister agencies
6. Police crisis intervention programs
7. Hot lines
8. Marriage and family courses in schools
9. Other

IV. GENERAL CRIMINAL INFORMATION
A. High Fear Crimes

	Offenses		Offenses Cleared	
	1990	Present Year	1990	Present Year
1. Murder	____	____	____	____
2. Forcible rape	____	____	____	____
3. Aggravated assault	____	____	____	____
4. Robbery	____	____	____	____
5. Burglary	____	____	____	____

B. High Frequency Cases and Arrests

	Incidents Handled		Offenses		Offenses Cleared	
	1990	Present Year	1990	Present Year	1990	Present Year
1. Drunkenness	____	____	____	____	____	____
2. Theft/larceny	____	____	____	____	____	____
a. Felony	____	____	____	____	____	____
b. Misdemeanor	____	____	____	____	____	____
3. Disorderly Conduct (disturbing the peace)	____	____	____	____	____	____
4. Narcotic/drug laws	____	____	____	____	____	____
5. Drunk driving	____	____	____	____	____	____
6. Liquor laws	____	____	____	____	____	____
7. Auto theft	____	____	____	____	____	____
8. Runaway (juvenile)	____	____	____	____	____	____
9. Simple assault	____	____	____	____	____	____
10. Reckless driving	____	____	____	____	____	____
11. Malicious destruction vandalism	____	____	____	____	____	____
12. Missing persons	____	____	____	____	____	____
13. Disturbance calls	____	____	____	____	____	____
14. Drive by shootings	____	____	____	____	____	____

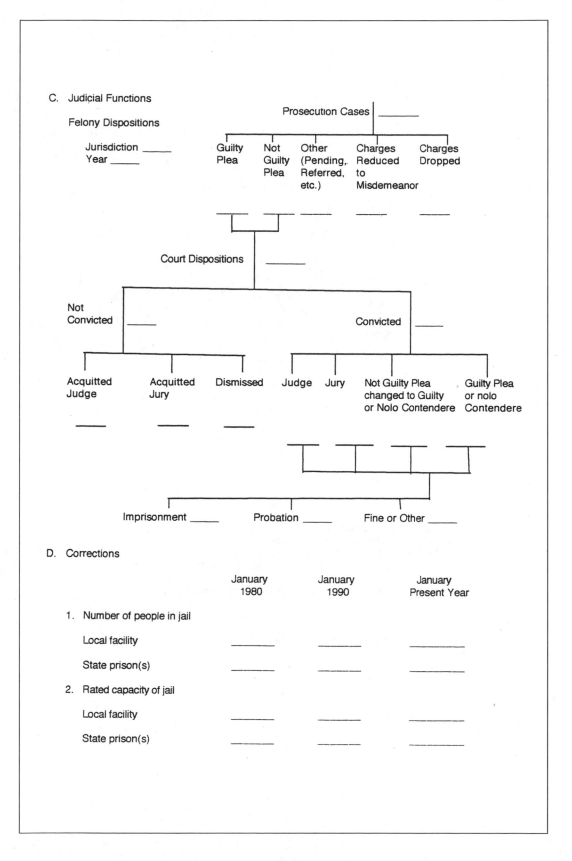

C. Judicial Functions

Felony Dispositions

Prosecution Cases _____

Jurisdiction _____
Year _____

| Guilty Plea | Not Guilty Plea | Other (Pending, Referred, etc.) | Charges Reduced to Misdemeanor | Charges Dropped |

Court Dispositions _____

Not Convicted _____   Convicted _____

| Acquitted Judge | Acquitted Jury | Dismissed | Judge | Jury | Not Guilty Plea changed to Guilty or Nolo Contendere | Guilty Plea or nolo Contendere |

Imprisonment _____   Probation _____   Fine or Other _____

D. Corrections

	January 1980	January 1990	January Present Year
1. Number of people in jail			
Local facility	_____	_____	_____
State prison(s)	_____	_____	_____
2. Rated capacity of jail			
Local facility	_____	_____	_____
State prison(s)	_____	_____	_____

E. Allocation of Correction Budget

	January 1980	January 1990	January Present year
State:			
1. Total correction budget	_____	_____	_____
2. Amount spent for maintenance	_____	_____	_____
3. Amount spent for new construction	_____	_____	_____
4. Amount spent for personnel	_____	_____	_____
5. Other	_____	_____	_____
Local:			
1. Total correction budget	_____	_____	_____
2. Amount spent for maintenance	_____	_____	_____
3. Amount spent for new construction	_____	_____	_____
4. Amount spent for personnel	_____	_____	_____
5. Other	_____	_____	_____

V. SOURCES OF INFORMATION

A. Government Agency Publications

1. U.S. Census Bureau Publications
   a. Number of Inhabitants (1980 and 1990 Census)
   b. Population Characteristics (1980 and 1990 Census)
   c. General Social and Economic Characteristics (1980 and 1990 Census)

2. Vital Statistics of the United States, Volume III - Marriage and Divorce

3. Crime in the United States, Uniform Crime Reports, FBI

4. Criminal Victimization in the United States
   A National Crime Survey Report, National Criminal Justice Information and Statistics Services

Sample Letter of Introduction

Hello. My name is _____, and I'm proud to introduce myself as your Community Policing Officer. I may be contacted by phone at _____. Community Policing is a new effort, not an old program warmed over. It is much more than just the idea of the old "beat cop." This new concept has as its basis the idea of direct, personalized services to our community.

Let me acquaint you with some of my responsibilities and duties:

1. Organize the resources of the police department, other agencies, and the community to reduce crime and solve neighborhood problems.
2. Conduct public education programs on crime prevention.
3. Maintain contact with citizens' groups operating within neighborhoods and involve them in planning, designing, and evaluating neighborhood crime prevention programs.
4. Patrol streets to strengthen lines of communication with citizens and prevent crime and delinquency.
5. Receive complaints and requests for service from residents.
6. Attend neighborhood block clubs and offer services.
7. Attend school advisory councils in assigned areas.
8. Investigate crimes.
9. Prepare written crime prevention material for community newsletters.

If you need the police in an EMERGENCY, call Police Radio at _____.
If you have other crime or community problems, however, please call me at my local office at _____. I look forward to getting to know you on a first-name basis, and to meeting the needs of this community.

My primary goal as a Community Policing Officer is to help organize resources to prevent and reduce crime. Please work with me to accomplish these goals. By working together, we will continue to make our community a better place to live.

Sincerely,

_____
Your Community Policing Officer

Sample Letter of Routine Property Check

Date: _____

Hello, I'm your Community Policing Officer, and my name is _____ _____. I stopped by to check your property today at _____ a.m./p.m. I would especially like to mention to you:

_____

_____

_____

_____

_____

_____

_____

I serve as your personal Community Policing Officer. My sergeant is also available in this area to serve you. If we can help you with anything in particular, please contact me at my local phone at _____. Leave a message if I'm out, or call the central patrol office at _____.

_____

Your Community Policing Officer

Sample Community Input Questionnaire

This is an anonymous questionnaire produced by your police department. Its purpose is to determine the concerns and views of the residents of the city about their police department and how it could best serve the needs of the community. Your views concerning the following are of utmost importance. Remember, your responses are completely anonymous. Please answer each question carefully, and return the completed questionnaire in the enclosed envelope or give it to your community policing officer if you so desire.

1. What activities would you like to see your police department concentrate their efforts on? (Obviously the police will deal with the most serious crimes like homicide and rape.)

Check only one column for each item:	1 Much Attention	2 Attention Sometimes	3 Little Attention
How much priority should the police give to:			
a) Burglaries	_____	_____	_____
b) Property destruction	_____	_____	_____
c) Auto thefts	_____	_____	_____
d) Traffic law violations	_____	_____	_____
e) Robberies	_____	_____	_____
f) Prostitution	_____	_____	_____
g) Juvenile curfew violations	_____	_____	_____
h) Larceny	_____	_____	_____
i) Loud parties	_____	_____	_____
j) Drug law violations	_____	_____	_____
k) Abandoned cars	_____	_____	_____
l) Gambling	_____	_____	_____
m) Assaults	_____	_____	_____
n) Other—specify ( )	_____	_____	_____

2. Please prioritize the offenses that you would like your police department to work on, by marking a number 1 for the highest priority, 2 for the next priority and so on.
    a) Burglaries _____
    b) Property destruction _____
    c) Auto thefts _____
    d) Traffic law violations _____
    e) Robberies _____
    f) Prostitution _____
    g) Juvenile curfew violations _____
    h) Larceny _____
    i) Loud parties _____
    j) Drug law violations _____
    k) Abandoned cars _____
    l) Gambling _____
    m) Assaults _____
    n) Other—specify (   ) _____

3. The following is a list of service types of activities performed by your police department. Which of these do you feel are most important? Check only six (6).
   a) Pick up found property _____
   b) Home security checks for vacationers _____
   c) Assist people locked out of their cars _____
   d) Investigation of all vehicle accidents _____
   e) Deliver personal messages _____
   f) School truancy checks _____
   g) Vehicle safety checks _____
   h) Business building security inspections _____
   i) Teaching grades K-6 pedestrian safety _____
   j) Teaching rape prevention programs _____
   k) Checking the welfare of senior citizens _____
   l) Assisting people locked out of their homes _____
   m) Assisting stranded motorists _____

4. What is your responsibility as a citizen in relation to dealing with crime? (Check one or more.)
   a) Avoiding involvement with victim _____
   b) Assisting victim needing help _____
   c) Reporting suspicious activity _____
   d) Avoiding involvement with police _____
   e) Reporting crime _____
   f) Assisting police officers needing help _____

5. With which of the following offenses would you be willing to help the police? (Check as many as you want.)
   a) Burglaries _____
   b) Property destruction _____
   c) Auto thefts _____
   d) Traffic law violations _____
   e) Robberies _____
   f) Prostitution _____
   g) Juvenile curfew violations _____
   h) Larceny _____
   i) Loud parties _____
   j) Drug law violations _____
   k) Abandoned cars _____
   l) Gambling _____
   m) Assaults _____
   n) Other—specify (   ) _____

6. Are you willing to be a volunteer to help your community policing officer improve the quality of life in your neighborhood?

    Yes _____   No _____

7. Do you know the names of neighborhood leaders who are respected and active in neighborhood affairs? If the answer is yes, please list the names.

    Yes _____   No_____

    _____

    _____

    _____

8. Were you the victim of crime within the last two years?

    Yes _____   No _____

    If the answer was yes to question number eight (8), did you report the crime?

    Yes _____   No _____

    For analysis purposes, please indicate your sex/gender.

    Male _____   Female _____

Now that you have completed this questionnaire, please enclose it in the envelope and place it in any mailbox. When the questionnaires have been tallied, the results will be announced publicly by the police department. Your response will be helpful in setting police priorities and policies. Thank you for your cooperation.

Sample Questionnaire to Determine Community Policing Effectiveness

Name _____ Phone _____ Beat Area # _____

Address _____ Age _____ Gender _____ Race _____

Is this a residence or business address? _____

Number of years you have been in the neighborhood _____ Date _____

1. Are you aware of the community policing effort in this neighborhood?
2. How did you become aware of it?
3. Do you know what the community officer is required to do by the police department?
4. What do you, as a citizen, expect of the community policing officer in your neighborhood?
5. Are you satisfied personally with community policing officer in your neighborhood?
6. Have you personally seen or spoken to the community policing officer?
7. How often?
8. What is his/her name? (What does he/she look like?)
9. Is the crime problem more or less serious in your neighborhood as compared to other neighborhoods in the city? What types of crimes are you most concerned about?
10. Has the community policing effort lowered the crime rate in your neighborhood?
11. Do you know of crime in the neighborhood that has gone unreported? How much?
12. Has the community officer encouraged citizens to report crime and become involved in crime prevention programs?
13. Have you been the victim of a crime in the past three years? If yes, did you report it? If you did not report it, why not?
14. Have you talked with neighbors about community policing?
15. What is their opinion of it?
16. Are you aware of any neighborhood projects that your community policing officer is involved in, in cooperation with neighborhood residents?
17. Do you have suggestions as to how the community policing effort can be improved?
18. Has the community policing effort increased the safety of women, the elderly, and young people?
19. How can the protection for women, the elderly, and children be improved?
20. Do you feel safer because of the community policing effort?
21. On the items below, state who is more effective, motorized patrol officers or community policing officers (use MP or CP).

    a. preventing crime _____
    b. encouraging citizen to help protect themselves _____
    c. responding to complaints _____
    d. investigating the circumstances of crime _____
    e. working with juveniles _____
    f. following up on complaints _____

Sample Work Plan for Community Policing Officers

My main objectives for the week of _____ through _____ are:

1.

2.

3.

Officer _____

Sergeant _____

_____

Date _____

Evaluation of progress toward above three objectives:

1.

2.

3.

Officer _____

Sergeant _____

Sample Union-Management Agreement

Community Services Bureau Flexible Work Week Understanding

Whereas, certain functions of the Community Services Bureau are better facilitated on other than a regular eight-hour-a-day basis, and

Whereas, it is the desire of said bureau to afford its employees convenient utilization of off-duty hours as well as provide for maximum efficiency in bureau activities:

It is therefore agreed between the Community Services Bureau and the undersigned employees to waive Article 17, Section 1 and Article 11, Section 3 of the agreement between the City of Flint and Teamsters Local 214 and Public Act of the State of Michigan, 379, M.P.A. as outlined below:

1. The undersigned employed may be scheduled for more or less than eight (8) hours on any day provided, however, such hours shall be consecutive and the cumulative amount shall not exceed or be less than 80 hours in a pay period.

2. This agreement shall not constitute a waiver of the days off scheduling as outlined in Article 11, Section 3.

3. Only scheduled hours in excess of 80 hours in a pay period will be considered overtime.

4. This agreement is in no way construed as circumventing the collective bargaining agreement between the City of Flint and Teamsters Local 214, and said agreement may be terminated at any time on the part of the City and/or Union or by mutual consent. This agreement is without precedence.

_____
Deputy Chief
Community Services Bureau

_____
Chief Union Steward
Teamsters Local 214

Additional Resources

Allen, D. & Maxfield, M. (1983). "Judging Police Performance: View and Behaviors of Patrol Officers." In R. Bennett (ed.) *Police at Work: Policy Issues and Analysis.* Beverly Hills, CA: Sage Publications.

Alpert, G. & Dunham, R. (1988). *Policing Multi-Ethnic Neighborhoods: The Miami Study and Finding for Law Enforcement in the United States.* New York, NY: Greenwood Press.

Alpert, G. & Dunham, R. (1989). "Community Policing." In R. Dunham & G. Alpert (eds.) *Critical Issues in Policing: Contemporary Readings.* Prospect Heights, IL: Waveland Press.

Angel, J. (1971). "Toward an Alternative to the Classic Police Organizational Arrangements: A Democratic Model." *Criminology,* 9, pp. 186-206.

Banas, D. & Trojanowicz, R. (1985). *Uniform Crime Reporting and Community Policing: An Historical Perspective.* East Lansing, MI: Michigan State University, National Neighborhood Foot Patrol Center.

Barnett, C. & Bowers, R. (1990). "Community Policing, the New Model for the Way the Police Do Their Job." *Public Management,* 72, pp. 2-6.

Bayley, D. (1989). *A Model of Community Policing: The Singapore Force Story.* Washington, DC: National Institute of Justice.

Brandstatter, A. (1989). *Reinventing the Wheel in Police Work: A Sense of History.* East Lansing, MI: Michigan State University, National Center for Community Policing.

Belknap, J., Morash, M. & Trojanowicz, R. (1986). *Implementing a Community Policing Model for Work with Juveniles: An Exploratory Study.* East Lansing, MI: Michigan State University, National Neighborhood Foot Patrol Center.

Bennett, R. & Baxter, S. (1985). "Police and Community Participation in Anti-Crime Programs." In J. Fyfe (ed.) *Police Management Today: Issues and Case Studies.* Washington, DC: International City/County Management Association.

Bittner, E. (1967). "The Police on Skid-Row: A Study of Peace Keeping." *American Sociological Review,* 32, pp. 699-715.

Bittner, E. (1970). *The Functions of Police in Modern Society.* Washington, DC: National Institute of Mental Health.

Bowers, J. & Hirsch, J. (1987). "The Impact of Foot Patrol Staffing on Crime and Disorder in Boston: An Unmet Promise." *American Journal of Police,* 6(1), pp. 17-44.

Boydstun, J. & Sherry, M. (1975). *San Diego Community Profile: Final Report.* Washington, DC: Police Foundation.

Bradshaw, R. (ed.) (1990). *Reno Police Department's Community Oriented Policing—Plus.* Reno, NV: Reno Police Department.

Braiden, C. (1986). "Bank Robberies and Stolen Bikes." *Canadian Police College Journal,* 10(1).

Bright, J. (1991). "Crime Prevention: The British Experience." In K. Stenson & D. Cowell (eds.) *The Politics of Crime Control,* pp. 62-86. London, UK: Sage Publications.

Brown, D. & Iles, S. (1985). *Community Constable: A Study of a Policing Initiative.* London, UK: Home Office Research and Planning Unit.

Brown, G. & MacNeil, A. (1980). *Police Patrol in Victoria: The Prahran Patrol Evaluation.* Melbourne, Australia: Victoria Police.

Brown, L. (1985). "Community-Policing Power Sharing." In W. Geller (ed.) *Police Leadership in America: Crisis and Opportunity.* New York, NY: Praeger.

Brown, L. (1989). "Community Policing: A Practical Guide for Police Officers." *Perspectives on Policing,* 12, (NCJ 118001) Washington, DC: National Institute of Justice.

Brown, L. (1991). *Policing New York City in the 1990's: The Strategy for Community Policing.* New York, NY: New York City Police Department.

Brown, L. (1991). "Community Policing: Its Time has Come." *Police Chief,* 58(9), p. 6.

Brown, L. & Wycoff, M. (1987). "Policing Houston: Reducing Fear and Improving Service." *Crime and Delinquency,* 33, pp. 71-89.

Caprara, D & Alexander, B. (1989). *Empowering Residents of Public Housing: A Resource Guide for Resident Management.* Washington, DC: National Center for Neighborhood Enterprise.

Cirel, P., Evans, P., McGillis, D., & Witcomb, D. (1977). *Community Crime Prevention Program, Seattle, Washington: An Exemplary Project.* Washington, DC: U.S. Department of Justice, National Institute of Justice.

Clairmont, D. (1990). *To the Forefront: Community-Based Zone Policing in Halifax.* Ottawa, Ontario: Canadian Police College, The Royal Canadian Mounted Police.

Clairmont, D. (1991). "Community-Based Policing: Implementation and Input." *Canadian Journal of Criminology,* 33, (3-4), pp. 469-484.

Clarke, R. (1983). "Situational Crime Prevention: Its Theoretical Basis and Practical Scope." In M. Tonry & N. Morris (eds.) *Crime and Justice: An Annual Review of Research,* 4. Chicago, IL: University of Chicago Press.

Clarke, R. (1992). *Situational Crime Prevention: Successful Case Studies.* Albany, NY: Harrow and Heston, Publishers.

Clarke, R. & Cornis, D. (1985). "Modeling Offenders' Decisions: A Framework for Research and Policy." In M. Tonry & N. Morris (eds.) *Crime and Justice: An Annual Review of Research,* 6. Chicago, IL: University of Chicago Press.

Clifton, W. (1987). *Convenience Store Robberies in Gainsville, Florida: An Intervention Strategy by the Gainsville Police Department.* Gainsville, FL: Gainsville Police Department.

Cohen, L. & Felson, M. (1979). "Social Change and Crime Rate Trends: A Routine Activity Approach." *American Sociological Review,* 44, pp. 588-605.

Community Relations Service (1987). *Principles of Good Policing: Avoiding Violence Between Police and Citizens.* Washington, DC: U.S. Department of Justice.

Connors, E. & Webster, B. (1992). "Police, Drugs, and Public Housing." *Research in Brief,* Washington, DC: National Institute of Justice.

Cordner, G. (1985). "The Baltimore County Citizen Oriented Police Enforcement (COPE) Project: Final Evaluation." Final report to the Florence V. Burden Foundation. Baltimore, MD: Criminal Justice Department, University of Baltimore.

Cordner, G. (1986). "Fear of Crime and the Police: An Evaluation of a Fear-Reduction Strategy." *Journal of Police Science and Administration,* 14, pp. 223-233.

Cordner, G. (1988). "A Problem-Oriented Approach to Community-Oriented Policing." In J. Greene & S. Mastrofski (eds.) *Community Policing: Rhetoric or Reality.* New York, NY: Praeger.

Cordner, G., Marenin, O. & Murphy, J. (1986). "Police Responsiveness to Community Norms." *American Journal of Police,* 5(2), pp. 83-107.

Couper, D. (1991). "The Customer Is Always Right." *Police Chief,* 58, pp. 17-23.

Couper, D. & Lobitz, S. (1991). "The Customer Is Always Right: Applying Vision, Leadership and Problem-Solving Method to Community Policing." *Police Chief,* 58, pp. 16-23.

Couper, D. & Lobitz, S. (1991). *Quality Policing: The Madison Experience.* Washington, DC: Police Executive Research Forum.

Currie, E. (1985). *Confronting Crime: An American Challenge.* New York, NY: Pantheon Books.

Davis. R. (1985). "Organizing the Community for Improving Policing." In W. Geller (ed.) *Police Leadership in America: Crisis and Opportunity.* New York, NY: Praeger.

Doone, P. (1989). "Potential Impacts of Community Policing on Criminal Investigation Strategies." In W. Young and N. Cameron (eds.) *Effectiveness and Change in Policing.* Study Series 33. Wellington, New Zealand: Institute of Criminology, Victoria University of Wellington.

Eck, J. (1989). *Police and Drug Control: A Home Field Advantage.* Washington, DC: Police Executive Research Forum.

Eck, J. (1990). "A Realistic Local Approach to Controlling Drug Harm." *Public Management,* 72(6), pp. 7-12.

Eck, J. & Spelman, W. (1987). "Who Ya Gonna Call? The Police as Problem Busters." *Crime and Delinquency,* 33, pp. 31-52.

Eck, J. & Spelman, W. (1987). *Problem Solving: Problem-Oriented Policing in Newport News.* Washington, DC: Police Executive Research Forum.

Eck, J. & Spelman, W. (1989). "A Problem-Oriented Approach to Police Service Delivery." In D. Kenny (ed.) *Police and Policing: Contemporary Issues.* New York, NY: Praeger.

Eck, J. & Williams, G. (1991). "Criminal Investigations." In W. Geller (ed.) *Local Government Police Management.* Washington, DC: International City/County Management Association.

Ent, C. & Hendricks, J. (1991). "Bicycle Patrol: A Community Policing Alternative." *Police Chief,* 58, pp. 58-60.

Esbensen, F. (1987). "Foot Patrol: Of What Value?" *American Journal of Police,* 6(1), pp. 45-66.

Farmer, M. (ed.) (1981). *Differential Police Response Strategies.* Washington, DC: Police Executive Research Forum.

Farrell, M. (1988). "The Development of the Community Patrol Officer Program: Community-Oriented Policing." In J. Greene & S. Mastrofski (eds.) *Community Policing: Rhetoric or Reality.* New York, NY: Praeger.

Fay, B. (1984). *Social Theory and Political Practice.* London, UK: George Allen & Unwin Publishers Ltd.

Fowler, F. & Mangione, T. (1983). *Neighborhood Crime, Fear and Social Control: A Second Look at the Hartford Program.* Washington, DC: U.S. Government Printing Office.

Fowler, F., McCalla, M. & Mangione, T. (1979). *Reducing Crime and Fear in the Urban Residential Area: The Planning and Evaluation of an Integrated Approach to Opportunity Reduction.* Boston, MA: Survey Research Program, University of Massachusetts.

Freeman, M. (1989). "Community-Oriented Policing." *MIS Report,* International City/County Management Association, 24, pp. 9.

Friedmann, R. (1987). "Citizens' Attitudes Toward the Police: Results from Experiment in Community Policing in Israel." *American Journal of Police,* 6(1), pp. 67-94.

George, A. (1992). *The First Line Supervisor's Perspective of Community Policing: A Participant Observation Study.* Unpublished paper for masters of science degree, Michigan State University, East Lansing, Michigan.

Goldstein, H. (1979). "Improving Policing: A Problem-Oriented Approach." *Crime and Delinquency,* 25, pp. 236-258.

Goldstein, H. (1977). *Policing a Free Society.* Cambridge, MA: Ballinger.

Goldstein, H. (1987). "Toward Community-Oriented Policing: Potential, Basic Requirements, and Threshold Question." *Crime and Delinquency,* 33, pp. 6-30.

Goldstein, H. (1990). *Problem-Oriented Policing.* New York, NY: McGraw Hill.

Goldstein, H. & Susmilch, C. (1981). *The Problem-Oriented Approach to Improving Police Service: A Description of the Project and an Elaboration of the Concept.* Madison, WI: Law School, University of Wisconsin.

Goldstein, H. & Susmilch, C. (1982). *Experimenting with the Problem-Oriented Approach to Improving Police Service: A Report and Some Reflections on Two Case Studies.* Madison, WI: Law School, University of Wisconsin.

Goldstein, H. & Susmilch, C. (1982). *The Repeat Sexual Offender in Madison: A Memorandum on the Problem and the Community's Response.* Madison, WI: Law School, University of Wisconsin.

Goldstein, H., Susmilch, C., Marlaire, C. & Scott, M. (1981). *The Drinking-Driver in Madison: A Study of the Problem and the Community's Response.* Madison, WI: Law School, University of Wisconsin.

Greenberg, S., Rohe, W. & Williams, J. (1982). *Safe and Secure Neighborhoods: Physical Characteristics and Informal Territorial Control in High and Low Crime Neighborhoods.* Washington, DC: U.S. Government Printing Office.

Greenberg, S., Rohe, W. & Williams, J. (1985). *Informal Citizen Action and Crime Prevention at the Neighborhood Level: Synthesis and Assessment of the Research.* Washington, DC: U.S. Government Printing Office.

Greene, J. (1987). "Foot Patrol and Community Policing: Past Practice and Future Prospects." *American Journal of Police,* 6(1), pp. 1-16.

Greene, J. & Mastrofski, S. (eds.) (1988). *Community Policing: Rhetoric or Reality.* New York, NY: Praeger.

Greene, J. & Taylor, R. (1988). "Community-Based Policing and Foot Patrol: Issues of Theory and Evaluation." In J. Greene & S. Mastrofski (eds.) *Community Policing: Rhetoric or Reality.* New York, NY: Praeger.

Guyot, D. (1991). "Problem-Oriented Policing Shines in the Stats." *PM: Public Management,* 73, (9), pp. 12-16.

Hartmann, F. (ed.) (1988). "Debating the Evolution of American Policing." *Perspectives on Policing,* 5, (NCJ 114214) Washington DC: National Institute of Justice.

Hartmann, F., Brown, L. & Stephens, D. (1988). *Community Policing: Would You Know It If You Saw It?* East Lansing, MI: Michigan State University, National Neighborhood Foot Patrol Center.

Hatry, H. & Greiner, J. (1986). *Improving the Use of Management by Objectives in Police Departments.* Washington, DC: Urban Institute.

Hatry, H. & Greiner, J. (1986). *Improving the Use of Quality Circles in Police Departments.* Washington DC: Urban Institute.

Hayeslip, D. & Cordner, G. (1987). "The Effects of Community-Oriented Patrol on Police Officer Attitudes." *American Journal of Police,* 6(1), pp. 95-119.

Higdon, R. & Huber, P. (1987). *How to Fight Fear: The Citizen Oriented Police Enforcement Program Package.* Washington, DC: Police Executive Research Forum.

Hoare, M., Stewart, G. & Purcell, C. (1984). *The Problem Oriented Approach: Four Pilot Studies.* London, UK: Metropolitan Police, Management Services Department.

Holland, L. (1985). "Police and the Community: The Detroit Administration Experience." *FBI Law Enforcement Bulletin,* 54, pp. 1-6.

Hoover, L. & Mader, E. (1990). "Attitudes of Police Chiefs Toward Private Sector Management Principles." *American Journal of Police, 9*, pp. 25-38.

Horne, P. (1991). "Not Just Old Wine in New Bottles: The Inextricable Relationship Between Crime Prevention and Community Policing." *Police Chief,* 58, pp. 24-30.

Hornick, J., Burrows, B., Tjosvold, I. & Phillips, D. (1989). *An Evaluation of the Neighborhood Foot Patrol Program of the Edmonton Police Service.* Edmonton, Alberta: Canadian Research Institute for Law and the Family.

International City/County Management Association. (1992). *Community-Oriented Policing: An Alternative Strategy.* Source Book. Washington, DC: International City/County Management Association.

Jacobs, J. (1961). *The Death and Life of Great American Cities.* New York, NY: Vintage.

Jeffrey, C. (1971). *Crime Prevention Through Environmental Design.* Beverly Hills, CA: Sage.

Johnson, P. (1984). "Police Community Relations: The Management Factor." *American Journal of Police, 3,* pp. 185-203.

Jones, L. (1989). "Community Oriented Policing." *Law and Order, 37,* pp. 25-27.

Karchmer, C. & Eck, J. (1991). "Drug Control." In W. Geller (ed.) *Local Government Police Management.* Washington, DC: International City/County Management Association.

Kelling, G. (1981). "Conclusions." In *The Newark Foot Patrol Experiment.* Washington, DC: Police Foundation.

Kelling, G. (1985). "Order Maintenance, the Quality of Urban Life, and Police: A Line of Argument." In W. Geller (ed.) *Police Leadership in America: Crisis and Opportunity.* New York, NY: Praeger.

Kelling, G. (1987). "Acquiring a Taste for Order: The Community and the Police." *Crime and Delinquency,* 33, pp. 90-102.

Kelling, G. (1988). "Police and Communities: The Quiet Revolution." *Perspectives on Policing,* 1, (NCJ 109955) Washington DC: National Institute of Justice.

Kelling, G. & Moore, M. (1988). "The Evolving Strategy of Policing." *Perspectives on Policing,* 4, Washington, DC: National Institute of Justice.

Kelling, G. & Stewart, J. (1989). "Neighborhoods and Police: The Maintenance of Civil Authority." *Perspective on Policing,* 10, (NCJ 115950) Washington DC: National Institute of Justice.

Kelling, G., Wasserman, R. & Williams, H. (1988). "Police Accountability and Community Policing." *Perspectives on Policing,* 7, (NCJ 114211) Washington DC: National Institute of Justice.

Kelling, G. & Wycoff, M. (1991). "Implementing Community Policing: The Administrative Problem." Paper prepared for the Executive Session on Policing Program in Criminal Justice Policy and Management. John F. Kennedy School of Government, Harvard University.

King, D. (1991). "Managing for Excellence." *FBI Law Enforcement Bulletin,* 60, pp. 20-21.

Klockars, C. (1985). "Order Maintenance, the Quality of Urban Life, and Police: A Different Line of Argument." In W. Geller (ed.) *Police Leadership in America: Crisis and Opportunity.* New York, NY: Praeger.

Klockars, C. (1988). "The Rhetoric of Community Policing." In J. Greene & S. Mastrofski (eds.) *Community Policing: Rhetoric or Reality*. New York, NY: Praeger.

Kobrin, S. & Schuerman, L. (1983). *Crime and Changing Neighborhoods: Executive Summary*. Los Angeles, CA: Social Science Research Institute, University of Southern California.

Kuykendal, J. & Roberg, R. (1982). "Mapping Police Organizational Change." *Criminology, 20*, pp. 241-256.

Larson, R. (1989). "The New Crime Stoppers." *Technology Review, 92*, pp. 26-31

Larson, R. (1990). *Rapid Response and Community Policing: Are They Really in Conflict?* East Lansing, MI: Michigan State University, National Center for Community Policing.

Lavrakas, P. (1985). "Citizen Self-Help and Neighborhood Crime Prevention Policy." In L. Curtis (ed.) *American Violence and Public Policy*. New Haven, CT: Yale University Press.

Lavrakas, P., Bennett, S. & Fisher, B. (1987). "The Neighborhood Anti-Crime Self-Help Program Evaluation: Some Preliminary Findings on Community Organization and Police Interaction." A paper presented at the annual meeting of the American Society of Criminology.

Lavrakas, P. & Kushmuk, J. (1986). "Evaluating Crime Prevention through Environmental Design: The Portland Commercial Demonstration Project." In D. Rosenbaum (ed.) *Community Crime Prevention: Does it Work?* Beverly Hills, CA: Sage.

Law Enforcement Assistance Administration. (1973). *National Advisory Commission on Criminal Justice Standards and Goals*. Washington DC: Department of Justice.

Leighton, B. (1991). "Visions of Community Policing: Rhetoric & Reality in Canada." *Canadian Journal of Criminology, 33*, (3-4), pp. 485-522.

Lewis, D. & Salem, G. (1985). *Fear of Crime: Incivility and the Production of a Social Problem*. New Brunswick, NJ: Transaction.

Loree, D. (1988). "Innovation and Change in a Regional Police Force." *Canadian Police College Journal, 12*, pp. 205-239.

Madison Police Department. (1988). *Planning Report for the Experimental Police District*. Madison, WI: Madison Police Department.

Manning, P. (1984). "Community Policing." *American Journal of Police, 3*, pp. 205-227.

Manning, P. (1988). "Community Policing as a Drama of Control." In J. Greene & S. Mastrofski (eds.) *Community Policing: Rhetoric or Reality*. New York, NY: Praeger.

Manning, P. (1989). "Community Policing." In R. Dunham & G. Alpert (eds.) *Critical Issues in Policing*. Prospect Heights, IL: Waveland Press.

Marenin, O. (1989). "The Utility of Community Needs Surveys in Community Policing." *Police Studies, 12*, pp. 73-81.

Marx, G. (1989). "Commentary: Some Trends and Issues in Citizen Involvement in the Law Enforcement Process." *Crime and Delinquency, 35*, pp. 500-519.

Mastrofski, S. (1983). "Police Knowledge of the Patrol Beat: A Performance Measure." In R. Bennett (ed.) *Police at Work: Policy Issues and Analysis.* Beverly Hills, CA: Sage Publications.

Mastrofski, S. (1988). "Community Policing as Reform: A Cautionary Tale." In J. Greene and S. Mastrofski (eds.) *Community Policing: Rhetoric or Reality.* New York, NY: Praeger.

Mastrofski, S. & Greene, J. (1991). "Community Policing and the Rule of Law." In D. Weisburd & C. Uchida (eds.) *The Changing Focus of Police Innovation: Problems of Law, Order and Community.* New York, NY:

McElroy, J., Cosgrove, C. & Sadd, S. (1989). "An Examination of the Community Patrol Officer Program (CPOP) in New York City." An unpublished report by the Vera Institute of Justice, New York.

McKnight, J. (n.d.). *The Future of Low-Income Neighborhoods and the People who Reside There: A Capacity-Oriented Strategy for Neighborhood Development.* Flint, MI: Charles Stewart Mott Foundation.

Meese, E. (1991). "Community Policing and the Police Officer." A paper prepared for the Executive Session on Policing Program in Criminal Justice Policy and Management. John F. Kennedy School of Government, Harvard University.

Melancon, D. (1984). "Quality Circles: The Shape of Things to Come?" *Police Chief,* 51, pp. 54-56.

Ministry of the Solicitor General. (1990, Jan.). *Community Policing: Shaping the Future.* Toronto, Ontario: Queen's Printer of Ontario.

Mitchell, W. (1990). "Problem-Oriented Policing and Drug Enforcement in Newport News." *Public Management,* 72, pp. 13-16.

Moore, M. & Kelling, G. (1983). "To Serve and Protect: Learning Form Police History." *The Public Interest,* 70.

Moore, M. & Kleiman, M. (1989). "The Police and Drugs." *Perspectives on Policing,* 11, Washington DC: National Institute of Justice.

Moore, M. & Stephens, D. (1991). *Beyond Command and Control: The Strategic Management of Police Departments.* Washington, DC: Police Executive Research Forum.

Moore, M. & Trojanowicz, R. (1988). "Corporate Strategies for Policing." *Perspectives on Policing,* 6, (NCJ 114215) Washington DC: National Institute of Justice.

Moore, M. & Trojanowicz, R. (1988). "Policing and the Fear of Crime." *Perspectives on Policing,* 3, (NCJ 111459) Washington DC: National Institute of Justice.

Moore, M., Trojanowicz, R., & Kelling, G. (1989). "Crime and Policing." In J. Fyfe (ed.) *Police Practices in the '90's: Key Management Issues.* (pp. 31-54) Washington DC: International City Management Association. Also in *Perspectives on Policing,* 2. Washington DC: National Institute of Justice.

Murphy, C. (1988). "The Development, Impact, and Implications of Community Policing in Canada." In J. Greene & S. Mastrofski (eds.) *Community Policing: Rhetoric or Reality.* New York, NY: Praeger.

Murphy, C. (1990, Jan). "Problem-Oriented Policing." In Ministry of the Solicitor General (ed.) *Community Policing: Shaping the Future.* Toronto, Ontario: Queen's Printer for Ontario.

Murphy, C. & Muir, G. (1985). *Community-Based Policing: A Review of the Critical Issues.* Ottawa, Ontario: Solicitor General of Canada.

National Institute of Justice. (1992, August). "Community Policing." *National Institute of Justice Journal.*

New York City Police Department. (1988). *Community Patrol Officer Program: Problem-Solving Guide.* New York, NY: New York City Police Department.

Nielsen, R. & Steele, B. (1984). "Quality Circles: A Police Management Experiment." *Police Chief,* 51, pp. 52-53.

Norman, M. (1984). "Quality Circles: A Program to Improve Employee Attitudes and the Quality of Series." *Police Chief,* 51, pp. 46-49.

Oettmeier, T. & Bieck, W. (1987). *Developing a Police Style for Neighborhood Oriented Policing: Executive Session #1.* Houston, TX: Houston Police Department.

Oettmeier, T. & Bieck, W. (1989). *Integrating Investigative Operations through Neighborhood Oriented Policing: Executive Session #2.* Houston, TX: Houston Police Department.

Oettmeier, T. & Brown, L. (1988). "Developing a Neighborhood-Oriented Policing Style." In J. Greene & S. Mastrofski (eds.) *Community Policing: Rhetoric or Reality.* New York, NY: Praeger.

Osborn, R. (1980). "Policing in Tune with Society." *Police Studies,* 3, pp. 30-36.

Ostrom, E., Parks, R. & Whitaker, G. (1978). "Police Agency Size: Some Evidence on its Effects." *Police Studies,* 1, pp. 34-46.

Pate, A., Wycoff, M., Skogan, W. & Sherman, L. (1986). *Reducing Fear of Crime in Houston and Newark: A Summary Report.* Washington, DC: Police Foundation.

Owens, R. (nd). "COPS: Community Oriented Problem Solving." Oxnard, CA: Oxnard Police Department.

Parker, P. (1990). "POP vs. Drugs." *Police,* 14, pp. 34-37.

Parker, P. (1991). "Herman Goldstein: The Man Who Made Problem-Oriented Policing a Reality." *Police,* 15, pp. 10-12, 75.

Pate, A. (1989). "Community-Oriented Policing in Baltimore." In D. Kenney (ed.) *Police and Policing: Contemporary Issues.* New York, NY: Praeger.

Pate, A., Wycoff, M., Skogan, W. & Sherman, L. (1989). *Reducing Fear of Crime in Houston and Newark: A Summary Report.* Washington, DC: Police Foundation.

Payne, D. & Trojanowicz, R. (1985). *Performance Profiles of Foot versus Motor Officers.* East Lansing, MI: Michigan State University, National Neighborhood Foot Patrol Center.

Philadelphia Police Study Task Force (1987). *Philadelphia and its Police: Toward a New Partnership.* Philadelphia, PA: Philadelphia Police Study Task Force.

Police Executive Research Forum (1989). *Taking a Problem-Oriented Approach to Drugs: An Interim Report.* Washington, DC: Police Executive Research Forum.

Police Foundation (1981). *The Newark Foot Patrol Experiment.* Washington, DC: Police Foundation.

Poyner, B. (1980). *Street Attacks and their Environmental Settings.* London, UK: Tavistock Institute of Human Relations.

Radelet, L. (1986). *The Police and the Community.* (4th ed.). New York: McMillan Publishing.

Ramsay, M. (1982). *City-Centre Crime: The Scope for Situational Prevention,* Research and Planning Unit Paper 10. London, UK: Home Office.

Reinier, G., Greenlee, M. & Gibbens, M. *Crime Analysis in Support of Patrol.* National Evaluation Program: Phase I Report. Washington, DC: U.S. Government Printing Office.

Reiss, A. (1985). "Shaping and Serving the Community: The Role of the Police Chief Executive." In W. Geller (ed.) *Police Leadership in America: Crisis and Opportunity.* New York, NY: Praeger.

Reiss, A. & Tonry, M. (eds.) (1986). "Communities and Crime." *Crime and Justice,* 8. Chicago, IL: University of Chicago Press.

Riechers, L. & Roberg, R. (1990). "Community Policing: A Critical Review of Underlying Assumptions." *Journal of Police Science and Administration,* 17 (2), pp. 105-114.

Rosenbaum, D. (1987). "The Theory and Research Behind Neighborhood Watch: Is It a Sound Fear and Crime Reduction Strategy?" *Crime and Delinquency,* 33, pp. 103-134.

Rosenbaum, D. (ed.) (1989). *Community Crime Prevention: Does it Work?* Beverly Hills, CA: Sage.

Rosenbaum, D. (1989). "Community Crime Prevention: A Review of What Is Known." In D. Kenny (ed.) *Police and Policing: Contemporary Issues.* New York, NY: Praeger.

Rosenbaum, D. & Baumer, T. (1981). *Measuring Fear of Crime: A Set of Recommended Scales.* Evanston, IL: Westinghouse Evaluation Institute.

Rosenbaum, D. & Heath, L. (1990). "The 'Psycho-Logic' of Fear-Reduction and Crime-Prevention Programs." In J. Edwards, R. Tindale, L. Heath & E. Posavac (eds.) *Social Influence Processes and Prevention.* Social Psychological Applications to Social Issues—Volume I. New York, NY: Plenum Press.

Rosenbaum, D., Lewis, D. & Grant, J. (1985). *The Impact of Community Crime Prevention Programs in Chicago: Can Neighborhood Organizations Make a Difference?* Final report to the Ford Foundation. Chicago, IL: Department of Criminal Justice, University of Illinois, Chicago.

Schwartz, A. & Clarren, S. (1977). *The Cincinnati Team Policing Experiment: A Summary Report.* Washington, DC: Police Foundation.

Sensenbrenner, J. (1986). "Quality Comes to City Hall." *Harvard Business Review,* March-April.

Sherman, L. (1986). "Policing Communities: What Works?" In A. Reiss & M. Tonry (eds.) *Communities and Crime, Crime and Justice Annual,* Volume 8. Chicago, IL: University of Chicago Press.

Sherman, L. (1989). "Repeat Calls for Service: Policing the 'Hot Spots.'" In D. Kenney (ed.) *Police and Policing: Contemporary Issues.* New York, NY: Praeger.

Sherman, L. & Berk, R. (1984). "The Specific Deterrent Effects of Arrest for Domestic Assault." *American Sociological Review,* 49 (2), pp. 261-72.

Sherman, L., Gartin, P. & Buerger, M. (1989). "Hot Spots of Predatory Crime: Routine Activities and the Criminology of Place." *Criminology,* 27, pp. 27-55.

Sherman, L., Milton, C. & Kelly, T. (1973). *Team Policing: Seven Case Studies.* Washington, DC: Police Foundation.

Sill, P. (1991). "Community-Oriented Policing and Crime Prevention Training: A Must for the '90s." *Police Chief,* 58, pp. 56-57.

Skogan, W. (1987). "The Impact of Victimization on Fear." *Crime and Delinquency,* 33, pp. 135-154.

Skogan, W. (1990). *Disorder and Decline: Crime and the Spiral of Decay in American Neighborhoods.* New York, NY: Free Press.

Skolnick, J. (1973). "The Police and the Urban Ghetto." In A. Niederhoffer & A. Blumberg (eds.) *The Ambivalent Force: Perspective on the Police.* San Francisco, CA: Rinehart Press.

Skolnick, J. & Bayley, D. (1986). *The New Blue Line: Police Innovations in Six American Cities.* New York, NY: Free Press.

Skolnick, J. & Bayley, D. (1988). *Community Policing: Issues and Practice Around the World.* Washington, DC: National Institute of Justice.

Skolnick, J. & Bayley, D. (1988). "Theme and Variation in Community Policing." In M. Tonry & N. Morris (eds.) *Crime and Justice: A Review of Research,* Volume 8. Chicago, IL: University of Chicago Press.

Sloan, R., Trojanowicz, R. & Bucqueroux, B. (1992). *Basic Issues in Training: A Foundation for Community Policing.* East Lansing, MI: National Center for Community Policing Publishing.

Sower, C. (1957). *Community Involvement.* Glencoe, IL: Free Press.

Sparrow, M. (1988). "Implementing Community Policing." *Perspectives on Policing,* 9, (NCJ 114217), Washington, DC: National Institute of Justice.

Sparrow, M., Moore, M., & Kennedy, D. (1990). *Beyond 911.* New York, NY: Basic Books.

Spelman, W. & Eck, J. (1987). "Problem-Oriented Policing Bureaucracy." A paper presented to the annual meeting of the American Political Science Association.

Spelman, W. & Eck, J. (1987). "Problem-Oriented Policing." *Research in Brief,* January. Washington, DC: National Institute of Justice.

Spelman, W. & Eck, J. (1989). "The Police and Delivery of Local Governmental Services: A Problem Oriented Approach." In J. Fyfe (ed.) *Police Practices in the '90's: Key Management Issues,* pp. 55-72. Washington, DC: International City Management Association.

Spelman, W. & Eck, J. (1989). "Sitting Ducks, Ravenous Wolves, and Helping Hands: New Approaches to Urban Policing." *Public Affairs Comment.* Austin, TX: Lyndon Johnson School of Public Affairs, University of Texas, Austin.

Spergel, I. (1969). *Community Problem-Solving.* Chicago, IL: University of Chicago Press.

Stern, G. (1991). "Community Policing Six Years Later: What Have We Learned." *Law and Order,* 39, pp. 52-54.

Sykes, G. (1986). "Street Justice: A Moral Defense of Order Maintenance Policing." *Justice Quarterly,* 3, pp. 497-512.

Tafoya, W. (1990). "The Future of Policing." *FBI Law Enforcement Bulletin,* 59(1), pp. 13-17.

Taft, P. (1986). *Fighting Fear: The Baltimore County COPE Project.* Washington, DC: Police Executive Research Forum.

Talarico, S. & Swanson, Jr., C. (1980). "The Limits of Team Policing?" *Police Studies,* 3, pp. 21-29.

Taub, R., Taylor, D. & Dunham, J. (1982). *Crime, Fear of Crime, and the Deterioration of Urban Neighborhoods: Executive Summary.* Washington, DC: U.S. Government Printing Office.

Taub, R., Taylor, D. & Dunham, J. (1984). *Patterns of Neighborhood Change: Race and Crime in Urban America.* Chicago, IL: University of Chicago Press.

Taylor, R., Gottfredson, S. & Bower, S. (1980). "The Defensibility of Defensible Space." In T. Hirschi & M. Gottfredson (eds.) *Understanding Crime.* Beverly Hills, CA: Sage.

Taylor, R., Gottfredson, S. & Schumaker, S. (1984). *Neighborhood Response to Disorder.* Baltimore, MD: Center for Metropolitan Planning and Research, Johns Hopkins University.

Toch, H. (1980). "Mobilizing Police Expertise." In L. Sherman (ed.) *The Police and Violence: The Annals of the American Academy of Political and Social Science,* 452, pp. 53-62.

Toch, H. & Grant, J. (1991). *Police as Problem Solvers.* New York, NY: Plenum Press.

Tomovich, V. & Loree, D. (1989). "In Search of New Directions: Policing in Niagara Region." *Canadian Police College Journal,* 13, pp. 29-54.

Tonry, M. & Morris, N. (eds.) (1988). *Crime and Justice: A Review of Research,* Volume 8. Chicago, IL: University of Chicago Press.

Trojanowicz, R. (1972). "Police-Community Relations." *Criminology,* 9, pp. 401-423.

Trojanowicz, R. (1982). *An Evaluation of the Neighborhood Foot Patrol Program in Flint, Michigan.* East Lansing, MI: Michigan State University, National Neighborhood Foot Patrol Center.

Trojanowicz, R. (1983). "An Evaluation of a Neighborhood Foot Patrol Program." *Journal of Police Science and Administration,* 11, pp. 410-419.

Trojanowicz, R. (1984). "Foot Patrol: Some Problem Areas." *Police Chief,* 51, pp. 47-49.

Trojanowicz, R. (1989). *Preventing Civil Disturbances: A Community Policing Approach.* East Lansing, MI: Michigan State University, National Center for Community Policing.

Trojanowicz, R. & Banas, D. (1985). *The Impact of Foot Patrol on Black and White Perceptions of Policing.* East Lansing, MI: Michigan State University, National Neighborhood Foot Patrol Center.

Trojanowicz, R. & Banas, D. (1985). *Perceptions of Safety: A Comparison of Foot Patrol versus Motor Patrol Officers.* East Lansing, MI: Michigan State University, National Neighborhood Foot Patrol Center.

Trojanowicz, R. & Banas, D. (1985). *Job Satisfaction: A Comparison of Foot Patrol versus Motor Patrol Officers.* East Lansing, MI: Michigan State University, National Neighborhood Foot Patrol Center.

Trojanowicz, R. & Belknap, J. (1986). *Community Policing: Training Issues.* East Lansing, MI: Michigan State University, National Neighborhood Foot Patrol Center.

Trojanowicz, R. & Bucqueroux, B. (1990). *Community Policing: A Contemporary Perspective.* Cincinnati, OH: Anderson Publishing Co.

Trojanowicz, R. & Bucqueroux, B. (1991). *Community Policing and the Challenge of Diversity.* East Lansing, MI: Michigan State University, National Center for Community Policing.

Trojanowicz, R. & Bucqueroux, B. (1992). *Toward Development of Meaningful and Effective Performance Evaluations.* East Lansing, MI: Michigan State University, National Center for Community Policing.

Trojanowicz, R., Bucqueroux, B., McLanus, T., & Sinclair, D. (1992). *The Neighborhood Network Center: Part One.* East Lansing, MI: Michigan State University, National Center for Community Policing.

Trojanowicz, R. & Carter, D. (1988). *The Philosophy and Role of Community Policing.* East Lansing, MI: Michigan State University, National Neighborhood Foot Patrol Center.

Trojanowicz, R. & Carter, D. (1990). "The Changing Face of America." *FBI Law Enforcement Bulletin,* 59, pp. 7-12.

Trojanowicz, R., Gleason, R., Pollard, B. & Sinclair, D. (1987). *Community Policing: Community Input into Police Policy-Making.* East Lansing, MI: Michigan State University, National Neighborhood Foot Patrol Center.

Trojanowicz, R. & Harden, H. (1985). *The Status of Contemporary Community Policing Programs.* East Lansing, MI: Michigan State University, National Neighborhood Foot Patrol Center.

Trojanowicz, R. & Moore, M. (1988). *The Meaning of Community in Community Policing.* East Lansing, MI: Michigan State University, National Neighborhood Foot Patrol Center.

Trojanowicz, R. & Pollard, B. (1986). *Community Policing: The Line Officer's Perspective.* East Lansing, MI: Michigan State University, National Neighborhood Foot Patrol Center.

Trojanowicz, R., Pollard, B., Colgan, F. & Harden, H. (1986). *Community Policing Programs: A Twenty-Year View.* East Lansing, MI: Michigan State University, National Neighborhood Foot Patrol Center.

Trojanowicz, R., Steele, M. & Trojanowicz, S. (1986). *Community Policing: A Taxpayer's Perspective.* East Lansing, MI: Michigan State University, National Neighborhood Foot Patrol Center.

Trojanowicz, S. (1992). *Theory of Community Policing.* Unpublished thesis for masters of science degree, Michigan State University, East Lansing, MI.

Uchida, C., Frost, B. & Annan, S. (1990). *Modern Policing and the Control of Illegal Drugs: Testing New Strategies in Two American Cities, Summary Report.* Washington, DC: National Institute of Justice.

Vera Institute of Justice. (1988). *CPOP: Community Policing in Practice.* New York, NY: Vera Institute of Justice.

Vines, M. (1989). *Community and Law Enforcement Against Narcotics: The Dallas Police Department's 1989 Drug Initiative.* Dallas, TX: Dallas Police Department.

Wadman, R. & Olson, R. (1990). *Community Wellness: A New Theory of Policing.* Washington, DC: Police Executive Research Forum.

Walker, S. (1984). "'Broken Windows' and Fractured History: The Use and Misuse of History in Recent Police Patrol Analysis." *Justice Quarterly,* 1, pp. 75-90.

Wasserman, R. & Moore, M. (1988). "Values in Policing." *Perspective in Policing,* 8, Washington, DC: National Institute of Justice.

Weatheritt, M. (1988). "Community Policing: Rhetoric or Reality." In J. Greene & S. Mastrofski (eds.) *Community Policing: Rhetoric or Reality.* New York, NY: Praeger.

Webber, A. (1991). "Crime and Management: An Interview with New York City Police Commissioner Lee P. Brown." *Harvard Business Review,* 69, pp. 111-126.

Weick, K. (1984). "Small Wins: Redefining the Scale of Social Problems." *American Psychologist,* 39, pp. 40-49.

Weisborn, M., Lamb, H. & Drexler, A. (1974). *Improving Police Department Management through Problem-Solving Task Forces: A Case Study in Organization Development.* Reading, MA: Addison-Wesly.

Weisburn, D. & McElroy, J. (1988). "Enacting the CPO Role: Findings from the New York City Pilot Program in Community Policing." In J. Greene & S. Mastrofski (eds.) *Community Policing: Rhetoric or Reality.* New York, NY: Praeger.

Weisburn, D., McElroy, J. & Hardyman, P. (1988). "Challenges to Supervision in Community Policing: Observations on a Pilot Project." *American Journal of Police,* 7, pp. 29-59.

Weisel, D. (1990). "Playing the Home Field: A Problem-Oriented Approach to Drug Control." *American Journal of Police,* 9, pp. 75-95.

Weisel, D. (1990). *Tackling Drug Problems in Public Housing: A Guide for Police.* Washington, DC: Police Executive Research Forum.

Weston, J. (1991). "Community Policing: An Approach to Traffic Management." *Law and Order,* 39, pp. 32-36.

Williams, H. & Pate, A. (1987). "Returning to First Principles: Reducing the Fear of Crime in Newark." *Crime and Delinquency,* 33, pp. 53-70.

Williams, J. & Sloan, R. (1990). *Turning Concept into Practice: The Aurora, Colorado Story.* East Lansing, MI: Michigan State University, National Center for Community Policing.

Wilson, J. (1983). *Thinking About Crime.* New York: Basic Books.

Wilson, J. & Kelling, G. (1982, March). "Broken Windows." *Atlantic Monthly,* pp. 29-38.

Wilson, J. & Kelling, G. (1989, February). "Making Neighborhoods Safe." *Atlantic Monthly.* pp. 46-52.

Winkel, F. (1988). "The Police and Reducing Fear of Crime a Comparison of the Crime-Centered and the Quality of Life Approaches." *Police Studies,* 11, pp. 183-189.

Witte, J., Travis III, L. & Langworthy, R. (1990). "Participatory Management in Law Enforcement: Police Officer, Supervisor and Administrator Perceptions." *American Journal of Police,* 9, pp. 1-24.

Wycoff, M. (1988). "The Benefits of Community Policing: Evidence and Conjecture." In J. Greene & S. Mastrofski (eds.) *Community Policing: Rhetoric or Reality.* New York, NY: Praeger.

Wycoff, M. & Manning, P. (1983). "The Police and Crime Control." In G. Whitaker & C. Phillips (eds.) *Evaluating Performance of Criminal Justice Agencies,* pp. 15-32. Beverly Hills, CA: Sage Publications.

Yin, R. (1986). "Community Crime Prevention: A Synthesis of Eleven Evaluations." In D. Rosenbaum (ed.) *Community Crime Prevention: Does it Work?* Beverly Hills, CA: Sage.

Young, J. (1991). "Left Realism and the Priorities of Crime Control." In K. Stenson & D. Cowell (eds.) *The Politics of Crime Control,* pp 146-160. London, UK: Sage Publications.